The Girl from White Creek

From the author of *Waiting on Zapote Street*,
winner of the Latino Books Into Movies Award,
Drama TV Series category

Betty Viamontes

The Girl from White Creek

I dedicate this book to—

My mother, my beacon of light even after her death.

My beloved husband, for supporting my community involvement and writing career, for being the love of my life and my best friend.

My loyal readers, for reading my books and encouraging me to keep writing.

My mother-in-law Madeline and father-in-law Guillermo, for meeting with me for over two years to help me document their story. Thank you for your love and support.

The members of all the book clubs who so kindly have chosen to read *Waiting on Zapote Street, The Dance of the Rose, Candela's Secrets and Other Havana Stories,* and *Havana: A Son's Journey Home* for your group discussions.

Chapter 1 - Madeline

Narrator: Madeline

I MET HIM IN ARROYO BLANCO, a town no one wrote about, before time and politics erased it from existence, a town too immersed on surviving to see the storm coming. I was fourteen, but our different ages didn't matter in a place where girls got married by age fifteen.

When my parents, my little sister, and I visited the center of town, he watched me from across the road. Walking at my pace, he ignored the old street vendor who passed up and down the street selling refreshing, ice-cold orange and lemon *granizado* ("shaved ice"). My admirer's thin mustache and brawny body made him appear a few years older than I, but the intensity of his gaze captivated me. It drew me in. It bestowed upon him a mysterious and fearless appearance. He was so different from me, afraid of my own shadow.

One day, as he turned his head to look at me, he collided with a well-dressed couple coming in the other direction. While he apologized, I covered my mouth to conceal my giggles.

Chapter 1 - Madeline

For a while, he kept his distance, even on those occasions when I left my parents and my sister at the grocery store to visit the ice cream parlor with my best friend, Mirta. She was a plump girl, three years older than I, who had a round, happy face and a contagious smile. We treated each other like sisters and shared our innermost secrets with one another.

On a hot August afternoon of the year 1955, when the sun baked the railroad track that divided the main street, and women and girls walked in both directions fanning themselves with *abanicos*, I heard him speak for the first time, a subtle "good afternoon, miss," cautious and respectful. He had a deep, husky voice I found pleasant. At the time, Mirta and I were walking by a row of stores while discussing an article about Fidel Castro that appeared on the Bohemia Magazine. The young revolutionary once again dominated the news, after President Batista granted him amnesty, two years after Castro and his men attacked the Moncada Barracks in Santiago de Cuba.

"I think he's so handsome and courageous," Mirta said and sighed.

"My father doesn't trust him," I said. "He questions his motivations, and I trust my father's judgement."

"How can you say that? Everyone likes Castro. The people are with him."

As Mirta and I spoke, we didn't suspect the impact Castro's release would have for our town and Cuba, or how his actions would affect my life and that of the handsome man who had sparked my interest.

Chapter 1 - Madeline

When I heard my suitor's voice, Mirta and I stopped discussing the article and turned our heads. As my gaze met his, it struck me how small his brown eyes were in relation to his face. I didn't know then that he enjoyed singing, but he resembled a handsome tenor, like the ones I watched on my grandfather's black-and-white television set. His striking good looks, thick black hair, and wide shoulders—like those of the men who worked at my grandfather's farms—awakened in me new feelings that I didn't understand.

After he walked past us, Mirta gave me a slight push.

"He likes you!" she whispered.

"Who, me? He's too old for me."

"He's not *that* old. Didn't you see how he looked at you? He was eating you with his eyes!"

"Ah! I don't think so, but if he did, he should go find someone his own age."

For the first time, I hid my true thoughts from Mirta. I didn't know why I felt the need to hide them, I just did. We chuckled, but I hoped she was right.

"My boyfriend knows him," she said.

"He does? From where?"

"The boxing ring. They practice boxing together."

"Boxing is for animals," I said. Yet I found the mixture of roughness and kindness both intimidating and fascinating.

"I know his name," Mirta said, arching her eyebrows.

"You do? What is it?"

3

Chapter 1 - Madeline

"I knew it! You do like him. His name is Willy."

"I don't like him, and I don't like his name either."

We both laughed.

When after that encounter I didn't see Willy for two weekends, I thought he had lost interest. Perhaps it had been my shyness, or the outfit I wore—a white muslin blouse, pearl necklace, and polka-dot skirt—which I thought made me look too refined. Or maybe I was too skinny or not pretty enough.

I had deep-rooted insecurities, even though my father worked hard to give me the best education and comfortable lifestyle a young girl could have. Regardless of how many suitors I had, I didn't consider myself attractive. My chest was more developed than many girls my age, and sometimes grown men who came to our house to discuss business with my father stared at me in unwelcome ways. This angered my parents, and to conceal my body, my mother made me wear blouses with ruffles and fluffy skirts. This unwanted attention had a different impact on me than on other girls my age. I felt ashamed. It made me feel like a large black dot on white fabric.

My relationship with my mother also affected how I perceived myself. We weren't close during my childhood. She turned on a physical-punishment button as if turning on a light switch. I didn't understand why, but since I turned seven, she smacked me on the head every time she was angry.

Chapter 1 - Madeline

On the various occasions my father came home from work and found me under the bed crying, he knew she had hit me.

"Why did you hit her?" he would ask her.

"She's exaggerating. It wasn't like that. She was walking on the wet floor!"

That was one of the many reasons she invented, always making up excuses for her behavior.

"Please don't do it again," he would tell her.

My father told me that past experiences molded people, and for a while I wondered what secrets her past held that caused her to behave as she did. Her life had been an enigma for me. She didn't say much about herself, a quality I thought she inherited from my maternal grandmother.

Every time we visited *Abuela*, she cooked us delicious meals and watched me eat them with pride, but her eyes revealed the sadness of someone who had suffered too much. When it came to the past, she and my mother seemed to share the same code of silence—one only my father helped me crack.

A couple of months before my fourteenth birthday, my father began to share with me stories about Mamá's past that allowed me to piece things together. Understanding was my first step to forgiving.

My maternal grandparents, married as teenagers, had nine children—five boys and four girls. They lived off the land, happy, watching their children grow while they matured into the best parents one could ever have.

Chapter 1 - Madeline

When my grandfather turned forty, a mosquito bite on his leg became infected. His leg swelled, and by the time he decided to seek help, he couldn't walk, so a group of men had to carry him out of the farm on an improvised hammock. Less than an hour later, the men returned with his body.

My grandmother prepared my grandfather for burial and sent messages to the family, asking them to come pay their final respects. For the next two days, his children hardly left his side.

After the burial, Mamá, the youngest and closest to her father, didn't say a word for an entire week. She was seven years old then, the same age I was when she started to hit me. Losing him must have impacted her more than anyone realized.

One of my uncles told me later that even if Grandpa had made it to the hospital, he would've died. Penicillin didn't exist back then, and his leg was too far gone for amputation.

My grandmother, Amparo, never remarried. She did the best she could to keep the farm producing enough for the family, but without my grandfather's expertise, the crops began to die. Lack of appropriate nutrition stunted my mother's growth. The shortest of her siblings, Mamá measured only five feet—four inches shorter than I did when I became an adult. Although Mamá didn't inherit her father's height, she found comfort in having his green eyes and milky complexion.

My grandfather's premature death shook Mamá and Abuela to the core. A year later, my mother's nine-year-old sister died of septicemia. Mamá told my father that Abuela Amparo was never the same following the loss of her child. After working on the farm all day, Abuela sat in a wooden rocking chair on the porch and looked up at the sky. Sometimes, she spoke to her dead daughter and to her husband. None of her children ever asked her about her monologues. After all, they too had to find their own ways of dealing with grief.

While learning the truth about my mother helped me understand her better, having Mirta's friendship filled the void. Like an older sister, she talked to me about boys and shared with me the latest rumors plaguing Arroyo Blanco. She came across as a straight shooter. Once she said that my appearance led people to believe I never did any housework, but I did. My parents could afford to pay someone, yet my mother would tell my father:

"Why would I hire someone to do what I can do myself? Also, this is a good exercise for Madeline."

Mamá taught me to wax the varnished wood floors, a task I did once a month. I also helped her clean the grey front porch, which extended from one end of the house to the other.

I loved our house. Green pastures adorned its surroundings, and about one hundred meters from the front porch was the railroad track, the same one that went through the center of town. Mirta lived on the other side of the railroad track, near the mayor of our town.

Every morning, the sound of trains passing by and the singing of roosters awoke me. From the porch, I could see the people passing by on the dirt path on both sides of the railroad. They traveled

7

either by car, on a horse, on a bicycle, or on foot. Some of the trains took workers to sugarcane fields. Others picked up the cut sugarcane and transported it to the mill for processing. Once processed, it was distributed through Cuba and abroad.

I never saw skies as blue or trees and pastures as green as those of my town. Our town's creeks and rivers, combined with its fertile soils, provided the perfect setting for planting many types of trees, from guava and mangoes to coconut, so food abounded in those parts.

When I was growing up, I often practiced English with my father's North American bosses who visited the house to discuss business matters with him. As I sat in a rocking chair to read, I could hear the men in the dining room speaking in either broken Spanish or English. My private lessons allowed me to understand a few of the English words and to greet them in their native language. One of them, Mr. Dutch, told me once that Arroyo Blanco meant "White Creek" in English.

"White Creek," I repeated to commit it to memory. I liked the way the name of our town sounded in English.

Mr. Dutch was a tall, blond, red-faced man who towered over my father. He smiled when I greeted him in his native language.

"Keep learning English," he would tell me. "You never know when it will come in handy."

Years later, I would understand the wisdom of those words.

When I turned twelve, my father sent me to a day school to learn how to sew, cook, preserve food, and become a successful homemaker. He thought these skills would allow me to become a good wife one day.

"My daughter will never have to work for anyone," he told my mother proudly. "I want her to marry a good man who will care for her as much as I do."

My mother rolled her eyes.

"You spoil her too much," she said. "English tutors and now more classes? For what? I never needed so many classes, and I'm doing just fine."

My mother's opposition to these classes did not deter my father from paying for them; if anything, he became more determined to provide me with the best education he could afford.

Despite the occasional physical punishment my mother administered to me when I did something that angered her, I saw there was good within her. My father often told me that no one was all good or all bad, and the night I saw her drop to her knees to pray to the Virgin of Charity to cure me when, at age thirteen, my fever refused to go down allowed me to see the good within her. That evening, she stayed by my side, weeping and caressing me until I fell asleep. I also noticed how much she cared for my father.

The few times my father stayed home sick, Mamá made him chamomile tea with honey and lemon juice and applied cool towels on his head to bring the fever down. This constant dichotomy of goodness and meanness my mother displayed confused me as a child, but after a while, I accepted it. After all, I couldn't change her. No one could.

Chapter 1 - Madeline

Like my father used to say: a tree that grows
crooked never straightens.

Chapter 2 – Arroyo Blanco

Narrator: Madeline

For my parents, living in Arroyo Blanco became a source of pride for the decent and prosperous life they found there.

The creeks running through my town gave it its name and filled it with life. During the day, I could hear roosters crowing, horses galloping, and steam-engine trains whistling; then at night, the music of crickets and the sounds of the wind caressing the carob trees returned.

Arroyo Blanco had three thousand in-habitants and three physicians. A plethora of interesting characters added color to an other-wise quiet town, from the town's dentist to the two popular boxers. Its only dentist, Señor Vargas, had gained notoriety for shooting his girlfriend when he found her with another man. Upon finishing his jail sentence, he re-turned to his practice, but people said that an-yone needing to have a tooth extracted had to arrive in his office before ten. After that, he was too inebriated to work. The few people who didn't heed this advice, including one of my uncles, left the dentist's office missing the wrong tooth.

Arroyo Blanco had two meat stores and a handful of clothing and grocery shops, not remembered so much by their names but by who owned them, like the stores of Borrás, Cipriano, Gustavo Milanés, and Rafael Milanés. It also had one clinic. The nearest hospital was approximately thirteen kilometers away in the municipality of Santa Cruz del Sur. There were only two barbers, Mario Reynó and Pepín Ávalo.

A town surrounded by farms and sugarcane plantations and inhabited by hard-working families, Arroyo Blanco provided access to three main sources of income: the land, the port, or the two large sawmills (*aserraderos*).

In Arroyo Blanco, rumors roamed the streets, with prominent residents, like Migdalia, spreading them like wildfire in sugarcane fields. As a well-known midwife, Migdalia delivered most of the babies in town—including my little sister and me. She had chocolate skin and a kind smile, but what she had in baby-delivery skills, she lacked in attractiveness. During a time when interracial marriages were uncommon, Migdalia married a white Spanish descendant, causing shockwaves throughout the town.

Migdalia knew everyone. When she went from house to house delivering babies, she heard a lot of secrets and didn't mind sharing them all over town with people who told others.

Chapter 2 – Arroyo Blanco

Rumors were not the only entertainment in Arroyo Blanco. The town had two popular boxers and a baseball team. Every Sunday, men gathered at the baseball field and sat on bleachers five levels high to enjoy Materva and Jupiña soft drinks, pork sandwiches, and cotton candy. My father didn't attend the games. Not that he disliked baseball, but he preferred to spend his weekends with the family.

I seldom saw my father smile. Intelligent, introspective, and taller and thinner than most men in town, he inspired respect, a reason why he rose through the ranks at the company where he worked. The Americans trusted him. They considered him a natural-born leader. A worrier, like me, and so different from my mother that I often wondered why he married her. Perhaps someone as grounded and quiet as my father needed someone as talkative and dramatic as my mother.

Every day, even on weekends, he dressed in a long-sleeve shirt and dress pants. When he wasn't working or spending time with family, he was listening to the radio to keep up with the latest political news—the only way he had to learn about events taking place in the rest of the country.

Arroyo Blanco had no newspaper; the nearest one was published in the Ciudad de Camagüey, located a few kilometers away. Local stores sold the Bohemia Magazine, but by the time the most recent issues arrived in town, the stories were old. Not that much happened in Arroyo Blanco, except for one day, when a teenager became inebriated in front of the store of the Milanés family. His father heard about it from the neighbors. When he saw his son falling over and demanding more liquor, the father slapped him in the face, shaming him in front of the town's people. After that, the boy disappeared. A group of men, including some of my uncles, searched for him for days until they found him dead. He had drunk a bottle of "Tinta Rápida," a black liquid used to clean shoes. Everyone in Arroyo Blanco attended the boy's funeral.

The death of that boy marked the most significant event to affect the entire town in its recent history, but the peaceful nature of the town was not to last. A couple of years later, deep in the forests of the Sierra Maestra Mountains, to the east of Arroyo Blanco, events that would transform the town and my life would be set in motion.

.

Chapter 3 - Willy

Narrator: Willy

"Stop fighting!" Sarita, my oldest sister yelled from the front porch.

She called the names of some of my brothers, those who still lived at home:

"Julio, Rolo, Rigoberto, Leo! Come help me, please!"

Meanwhile, Enrique and I punched each other like two boxers in the ring. The sun cooked the fertile soil as I fought for my dignity. Above all, I was a man. No one, not even my older brothers, could get away with challenging my manhood. I tried to wrestle my brother to the ground and heard my mother's voice.

"Boys, you're going to kill each other. Stop for God's sake!"

"Enrique needs to learn not to laugh at me!"

I grabbed my brother around his torso and held on to him until we lost balance and fell on the dirt. However, the fall didn't stop the punches between us.

15

My sister kept screaming for my other brothers to help break up the fight. Adrenaline kept me going. I didn't feel pain or the blood trickling down when my knee hit a small rock. Moments later, two of the oldest ones ran over and separated us.

"Look at you! You should be ashamed of yourselves, fighting about a girl that *you*, Willy, don't even know!" Sarita yelled.

Behind her back, my brothers called her "the dictator" as my mother had given her super-rights over her younger siblings.

"It's not my fault!" I yelled. "He said that when I talked about Madeline, I looked like a ballerina playing the violin."

My other brothers started to laugh.

"It's not funny!" I said. "Now he knows what this ballerina can do."

"Fair enough, my little brother," said Enrique. "Those were some good punches. It looks like you mean business."

Enrique placed his arm around my shoulder.

"You'll be alright," he said.

We laughed and walked into the house with busted lips.

It was 1955, three years after General Fulgencio Batista appointed himself Cuba's president through a military coup. Apart from a gentlemen's house that caused the outrage of every wife in the towns of Cubitas—where I lived—and Arroyo Blanco—and after months of protests closed its doors—the plague of organized crime and gambling prevalent in Havana had not tarnished our towns.

Too busy to worry about the conditions brewing at the capital, which would later fuel the revolution, I, Willy Montes, spent three years away from my hometown training in agricultural sciences. Now, at age nineteen and ready to settle down, I didn't realize how out-of-my-reach the girl on whom I set my eyes was. I didn't know that her father worked as a high-level executive at the respectable Macareño Industrial Corporation of New York and would not allow someone like me to get close to his oldest daughter, his most precious possession.

My father was no executive, but he worked hard and taught his boys well. He owned a farm of five *caballerías*—roughly 166 acres—where he and my mother raised twelve children, nine boys and three girls. From our farm, far in the distance, where the sky embraced the land, the hills of Najasa stood guard, saluting the royal palm trees of the plains.

In addition to working on the farm, when cargo ships arrived at Puerto de Guayabal—located over an hour away—my father operated a crane that lifted bags of sugar into cargo ships while longshoremen carried the sacks from the trains to the port. Being a crane operator required precision but paid good money.

My father, or *Viejo*, as his sons called him, taught his boys how to plant vegetables,

17

milk cows, and raise livestock while the girls helped my mother care for the children, do house chores, and pick vegetables for the delicious meals my mother cooked for the family. In those times, we had no shortage of food, and my family didn't hesitate to share it with those less fortunate.

Sometimes, my father used his Jeep to carry bags of corn from local ranchers' farms to their customers and didn't charge the ranchers for his service, but his generosity didn't end there. There were no hotels in our town, and my parents allowed transient men needing a place to spend the night to bring their hammocks and sleep in our stable. My mother, too kindhearted to let them leave hungry, always fed them.

Mom also adopted a local family of four girls and two boys. Their mother had died during childbirth and their father, addicted to playing dominoes for money, didn't do much for them. Mom never criticized the father for neglecting his family. She said that different people coped with the loss of a loved one in different ways. Who was she to judge?

Viejo understood Mom's need to be a mother to everyone, but sometimes they argued about it because her generosity knew no boundaries. Mom resolved these arguments using the same method she used to win over everyone she met: through her cooking. Her tasty meals, which I was certain matched those of the best chefs in the world, gave her such a great reputation in town that Angelino

Guerra, a close relative of Fidel Castro and the only semi-famous person I knew, often came to my house to eat her turkey fricassee.

My mother loved to cook white, brown, and black beans, all grown in our farm. I thought her best dish was meat and potatoes stew—which had a mouth-watering smell of oregano, onions, crushed garlic, and cumin that would waft its way to the front porch. Her flavorful *ajiaco*—my oldest sister's favorite—consisted of a festive array of almost every vegetable we planted, like potatoes, yucca, *boniato*, and carrots, with chunks of beef or pork, and sautéed onions, peppers, garlic, and spices. When we were growing up, my mother smashed it all up and gave it to us as a thick soup that she claimed could wake the dead. Ajiaco, she thought, was the soul of our farm.

Mom believed her ajiaco healed my brother Enrique from diphtheria when he contracted it at age eight. The epidemic killed hundreds, but she knew from the moment he became ill that her cooking would bring him back to health.

Every morning, we got up at five. The boys milked thirty of our eighty cows. The other cows were either pregnant, or their calves consumed most of their milk. Mom strained the milk into glass bottles for my brothers and me to distribute to our customers. Once the customers emptied their liter of milk into their own containers, they returned the glass bottle to us for refilling the next morning.

19

Chapter 3 - Willy

We sold many of the bulls when they were two or three years old, the best age to make the most money from their sale. We kept the cows to replace the old ones, then sold those.

After we finished milking the cows, we washed our hands and gathered around the large cedar table in the dining room, which accommodated up to twenty people. My mother had already served breakfast by then, and the house smelled like freshly brewed coffee and buttered toast. Our breakfast included blood sausage, chorizo, and white cheese my sisters made. Sometimes, we had bacon and pork. Others, we had mullet roe, a delicacy like caviar. My father, a mullet fisherman, extracted the mass of eggs from a female fish. My mother rolled the roe and fried it. It was one of my favorite breakfast dishes.

As we sampled each of the selections, joy spread around the table. We didn't talk much, other than to compliment my mother for her cooking. We then returned to the farm, ready for another productive journey until lunch. Our workday ended around four each day, when once again we sat around the table for another scrumptious meal. That was our daily routine. Hard work and good food.

As my brothers and sisters became adults, they married and left the farm, something I too hoped to do one day. Each time one of us left, I could see in my parents' eyes a rare mix of pride and disappointment. However, I grew up hearing them say:

"We are raising our children for the world, not for us. That is the law of life."

Now that I had fallen in love with the most beautiful girl of Arroyo Blanco, I couldn't wait to marry her and leave the farm.

My brothers thought I had lost my mind. They said I needed to slow down and get to know her better, but since I saw her that sunny afternoon, I couldn't get my eyes off her.

The yellow glow of the sun caressed her unblemished face, and her white ballerina-style shoes stepped carefully over the shop-lined dirt road. The moment she turned her head in my direction without noticing me, I felt as if the sun were shining only for me.

Sarita thought the girl had put a spell on me. She said only that could explain my obsession. True or not, the grace with which she walked and the subtle movements of her head when she smiled owned my thoughts.

Refined and thin, with shoulder-length wavy-brown hair, she had a rose-colored smile that detained time. Her brown eyes shared the shade of the heartland and her gaze the purity of the town's creeks. She didn't look like someone who worked on a farm, feeding and milking cows or tending to the crops like I had done since my childhood. Rather, she reminded me of a fine jewel, only worn on special occasions.

For a while, I admired her from afar, trying to find the right moment to approach her, comforting myself by carving her smile in my memory and imagining the sweetness of her lips; however, each passing week made it more difficult to stay away.

I had dated some women in Arroyo Blanco, most of them older than I, and slept with a couple who had questionable morals. My brothers laughed at me because I shied away from those types of women. They said I had overly high standards. What if I did?

Her aura possessed me and filled me with determination. I knew I would not stop until I had her heart.

One hot afternoon, when she passed by the local bread store, I built the courage to approach her. For a moment, she glanced at me, and I saw Mirta give her a little push and tell her something I couldn't hear.

Mirta was dating my friend Billy, so I knew her from the times the two of them went to the movie theater together.

Madeline's name suited her well. Julio, my smartest brother, told me that her name was derived from Magdala, a village on the Sea of Galilee. In Aramaic, "magdala" meant "great" or "magnificent," and she was indeed magnificent.

After that encounter, I went into the bread store, bought a loaf of bread, and returned to the farm, happy she had noticed me.

My town of Cubitas, located 30 kilometers away from Arroyo Blanco had a bar, a couple of stores, and many family farms, the reason why most men my age preferred to travel to Arroyo Blanco. There I felt the most complete, but never more so than after I met Madeline.

Every night, at nine, the house of one of my uncles—who owned one of the two sawmills in Arroyo Blanco—would fill with neighbors who came from the surrounding area to listen to the popular radio soap-opera "Leonardo Moncada." After the program ended, everyone walked back to their houses, and a man who people called "Alfredo el loco" would yell "¡Hi-eeeeerro!" His voice could be heard all over town, signaling to the people it was time to go to sleep.

I never saw Madeline's family at my uncle's house. In fact, people speculated that her father had been one of the first ones in town to own a transistor radio. I didn't care about the economic position of Madeline's family. I wanted *her*.

After the fight, Enrique stopped bothering me. Not my mother. She didn't like Madeline for a different reason. She said I needed a strong woman to help me work at the farm, someone heavy like her who knew how to care for a man, not a weakling who knew nothing about hardship.

"That relationship will never last," she said.

I loved my mother and understood she wanted the best for her sons. I also knew no one or nothing would stop me from fighting for the most beautiful girl in Arroyo Blanco.

Chapter 4 – Tía Rosita

Narrator: Madeline

My parents, my little sister, and I had one family vacation each year, always to the same place. For an entire month, we stayed at my paternal grandfather's farm, which allowed me to spend time with my grandparents and their daughter Rosita, my favorite aunt.

The wife of a sergeant and the only aunt who could not conceive a child, she sometimes stayed at her parents' house while her husband worked on assignments in other parts of the country.

"I love you like a daughter," she used to tell me.

Every time Tía Rosita saw me at my grandfather's house, her maternal instincts took over. Although she didn't cook because my grandparents had maids, she catered to my every desire. Sometimes I thought that if I had asked her for a star, she would have found a way to bring it to me.

My grandfather owned a large black dog, Sultán, too filthy from running in the farm for me to get close to him, but he followed my grandfather everywhere he went. When I visited Grandpa's farm, Sultán sometimes came running towards me. I recoiled and looked at him like I didn't want him to get close. He then lowered his head and walked away, but Tía Rosita, having her child-like disposition, played ball with him from the porch, watching him run after it and bring it back to her full of dirt and drool.

Perhaps the juvenile restlessness Tía Rosita portrayed caused her to treat me as an equal, and not in the condescending way other adults did. Despite our closeness, I didn't tell her at first about my admirer, nor the letter he had sent me with Mirta two weeks after he first spoke to me, which brought a smile to my face.

Chapter 5- My Sweet Fifteen

Narrator: Madeline

As the day of my *quince años* approached—a day marking the passage from childhood to adulthood—my excitement grew. Like many girls in town, I had been anticipating this moment since my early childhood years. Planning for my *quinceañera* occupied most of the conversations between my parents during the two years leading up to my celebration. However, no one seemed happier about the upcoming event than Nancy, my five-year-old sister.

Since the day of Nancy's birth, I had been very close to her. When she was a baby, I changed her diapers, bathed her, and read her children's books. As she grew older, she loved it when I sang popular children's songs to her or stayed by her side when she was too scared to fall asleep.

Nancy sometimes feared a ghost would come into our room in the middle of the night and take her. I never understood what caused her to feel that way. Mamá said Nancy had

been born with a higher awareness of her surroundings, that she could see those who had
died and marched on to another world.

Nancy personified kindness and love. By
age three, she began picking up flowers from
the garden and bringing them to my mother
and me. One day, while I rocked her on the
porch and read her a story, she placed her
arms around my neck and looked into my eyes.

"Madeline, can you be my mami?" she
asked.

The tenderness with which she said
these words made my eyes glisten and brought
us even closer, creating a bond no one could
ever destroy.

The hazel eyes of my little sister grew big
each time the seamstress came to our house,
first to take my measurements for my fif-
teenth-birthday dress, and later for fittings.
Nancy danced in front of a mirror, acting as if
she were wearing a long dress. Despite the
turns our lives took after that day, the innocent smile of that beautiful girl always remained with me.

For my celebration, my mother compiled
a select list of invitees that included my father's bosses, their families, and handpicked
people in Arroyo Blanco, including the town's
mayor. When Mamá overheard Mirta tell me
she had invited Willy, she said in no uncertain
terms:

"Only guests *I* invited will come to this
party. Understood?"

My friend nodded and apologized. Mamá then began to question her about Willy, a long interrogation that led my mother to order me to stay away from him. Embarrassed, Mirta uninvited him.

Mamá's list of invitees included the teenage son a wealthy ranch owner. She hoped the two of us would get to know each other during my party. Although not perfect by her rigid standards, she said he was one of the handful of men in Arroyo Blanco whom she would allow me to marry. My father asked her to stop looking for a husband for me.

"She's still a child," he said.

Mamá crossed her arms and gave him *the look*. I knew then nothing would stop her. She must have told a friend about her plans to find me a husband, and our town's rumor mill must have done the rest because, somehow, Willy heard about it.

The day before my party, Mamá and one of my aunts spent hours decorating our house, paying attention to every detail, from the white tablecloth that covered our table to the garlands scattered throughout our home. Our house looked beautiful, although it wasn't *ours*. It belonged to the Macareño Industrial Corporation, and like all the others the company owned, it was painted light grey, with green doors and green window frames. It stood on top of a small hill, which allowed it to be seen from several kilometers away, but it never looked as vibrant and alive as on the day of my fifteenth birthday.

Chapter 5- My Sweet Fifteen

On the day of my celebration, while the house teemed with invitees and I was talking to one of my mother's friends, Mirta approached me and asked me to follow her with her eyes. I excused myself, and we went to a corner of the dining room. She looked at me without saying a word, and I gave her a questioning glance. She then scanned our surroundings and whispered in my ear:

"Willy has been driving by the house!"

I opened my eyes wide.

"Oh my God! My mother's going to kill him!"

I walked towards the front of the house, while our guests—pouring from the living room onto the large porch—mingled with one another.

Along my path, the women complemented my attire, which forced me to stop several times to listen to their remarks. My maternal grandmother too approached me, took my hand between hers, and gave me a tender look.

"You make me so proud. Look at you! My princess. My beautiful girl is all grown up."

I smiled and gave her hug.

"Thank you, Abuela."

I then heard my mother's voice calling her away. When she left my side, another woman joined me and started examining my dress. I wore a champagne-color ball gown, embellished with pearls, beads, and appliqués.

"Exquisite!" the woman said.

Chapter 5- My Sweet Fifteen

The two of us were standing between the front porch and the living room. As she continued praising my dress, in the corner of my eye, I noticed a Jeep approaching our house very slowly and then passing in front of it, only meters away from our porch.

I kept trying to divide my attention between the Jeep and the woman when I saw Willy in the driver's seat. While the woman analyzed every detail of my dress, Willy and I locked gazes. He became so distracted he didn't realize he had veered onto the grassy area. I covered my mouth with my hand and my eyes widened. At that moment, as he realized something was wrong, his eyes shifted, just before he hit the tree. A large ball of dust lifted in the air when he slammed the brakes, causing the guests to look in his direction. The growling, grinding noise caused all the eyes to focus on him. My hands turned clammy. I anxiously looked around, searching for my parents. I couldn't see them, but I felt I had to go back inside. It made sense to me at that time. After making sure he was fine, I excused myself and rushed back in, acting as if nothing had happened.

My party lasted all afternoon.

"A successful event," Mirta heard people say. Then my life continued, boring and simple, but now with a light of hope that things would soon change.

My mother would later hear about someone fitting Willy's description almost running into a tree and quiz me about the incident. For the first time in my life, I lied:

"I don't know what you're talking about," I said.

She stared at me for a long time, waiting for me to confess.

"Don't test me, Madeline," she said. I looked down and asked to be excused, feeling that the relationship between my mother and me would never change.

It didn't take long for my sister to see my mother's negative side and the way she sometimes treated me, from the yelling to the painful pinches. This raised in my sister the need to protect me. One afternoon, when I returned home half an hour late, I found my little sister waiting for me on the porch.

"Defend yourself, Madi!" Nancy said grabbing my hands. "Mom is waiting for you. She's mad! Defend yourself!"

The caring way she would tell me "defend yourself," being as little as she was back then, warmed my heart, and I promised myself to always protect her.

Chapter 6 - The Meeting

Narrator: Madeline

Watching my reflection in the mirror one day, I told myself that my childhood years were now behind me, and I needed to act more like an adult. To spend time away from the watchful eyes of my mother, I volunteered to pick up the mail from the post office, accompanied by my friend Mirta. This allowed me to have casual encounters with Willy, where we exchanged pleasantries, but nothing more as common decency standards prescribed my behavior. Decent girls could love only from a distance. Anything more required the approval of her parents.

One day, when public conversations didn't suffice, Willy arranged a meeting with me at Mirta's house that she volunteered to facilitate. To that end, she invited me to her cousin's birthday celebration. Because the invitation came from my friend and not her parents, my parents assumed they were not invited. At first, my mother didn't want me to go, but my father convinced her I was a responsible young woman with a good head on my shoulders. My mother allowed me to attend only after Mirta promised not to leave my side.

Upon my arrival that evening, Willy, who had been waiting for me by the side of the house, came over to greet us. Mirta gave me a mischievous stare. Moments later, she excused herself and joined her small group of relatives inside.

For the first time, Willy and I found ourselves alone. The glow of the moon and the yellowish light seeping through the window shutters illuminated the porch. Back then, in those country towns, few people had electricity. Those who did, like Mirta's parents and mine, used home generators, so apart from the handful of illuminated houses, darkness owned the surroundings.

"When you drove by my house the other day, you scared me half to death," I said.

He remained silent at first, his intense gaze roaming over me. I looked down, focusing on my pink dress and puffy skirt.

"You're so beautiful," he said.

I smiled and thanked him, evading his eyes. The odors of his musky cologne and *brillantina,* a product that men used to secure their hair in place and make it shine, filled my nostrils. From the corner of my eye, I noticed his strong hands and the long-sleeve shirt that made him appear more handsome than I remembered.

As I stroked my arm, a breeze that smelled like soil and fruit trees enveloped our bodies, and for a moment, I realized how lucky we were to live in this place, so peaceful, yet so full of life.

"I'm sorry I couldn't come your birthday party," he said. I saw him reach into his shirt pocket.

"Here's a birthday gift for you."

He handed me a folded piece of paper.

"What is it?"

"It's something I wrote, my first poem, so please don't laugh."

I unfolded it and read it in silence beneath the glow that escaped from the window.

To Madeline

If the love I have for you
could be expressed in a percentage
without a doubt, I would give it
one hundred percent.
You deserve it.

Perhaps others would give less
to leave some love for another,
not me, you're my one and only,
like you, there is no other.

I stifled a giggle. It was the worst poem I had ever read, but after seeing the way he looked at me, his anxious gaze when he asked me what I thought of it, I couldn't reveal my thoughts.

"It's beautiful," I said. "It is the nicest thing anyone has ever done for me."

"You deserve it," he said.

He gave me a satisfied smile that made him appear less intimidating, so I smiled back. He then leaned closer to me.

"Madeline, I'm sorry for meeting you this way. You are a decent young woman, and I don't intend any disrespect. You know I've fallen in love with you, and if you feel the same way about me, I would like to meet with your father and request his permission to visit you at home."

The quiet tone of his voice conveyed sincerity.

"I think we need to wait. Besides, my father is very protective of me, and I don't know how he would react."

"I'm not afraid of him or anyone," he said.

"How old are you?"

"Nineteen, miss. Do you think I'm too old?"

"No. I find boys my age childish."

"You act more mature than young ladies your age."

"Thank you."

"So, if I can't visit your house, how do we get to know each other? Would you like to be my girlfriend?"

"I think so," I said with a slight shrug.

"In that case, why can't you let me talk to your father?"

"I need more time," I said feeling terrified.

I had never dated anyone. I didn't understand what girlfriends were supposed to do or how they should act. I had read dozens of love stories by Corín Tellado, but it was one thing to read about couples in love, and quite another to experience it.

Suddenly, the front door opened, and Mirta came out carrying two plates, each with a slice of cake. She handed them to us without saying a word. Before she went back inside, she looked at me and smiled.

We both ate the cake in silence, while he appeared intrigued by the way I ate it. Its texture and flavor made me think of my mother's comments on the day of my party. She told my father that my cake had been the best one she had ever tasted. This one seemed to be of the same caliber, two layers of moistened heaven, divided by a layer of custard and pineapple, a delight for the senses. I wondered if the pleasure reflected on my face as I ate caused him to look at me with such intensity.

The cake didn't last long. We placed the empty plates on a small table and spoke a while longer. During a brief silence, he reached for my hand and took it within his. I could feel the roughness of hard work on his skin, and his touch sent a tingling sensation throughout my body.

"I need to go," I said, retrieving my hand.

"When can I see you again?"

"I don't know."

We remained silent again, standing in front of each other, my eyes focusing on my shoes and his.

Chapter 6 - The Meeting

I wasn't expecting what happened next. He came closer to me, placed his arms around me, and gave me a soft kiss on the cheek. I let him at first but then stepped back. I was so frightened by the way his kiss made me feel, I rushed towards the front door without looking at him and announced:

"Mirta, can you walk me home? It's late."

I stood by the half-opened door looking in and wiped my face with my hands, as if doing so would erase any evidence of the kiss.

"Did I offend you, miss?" he asked.

I shook my head and signaled him to hush.

"I'd like to see you again, and please think about letting me speak to your father."

I could feel my body trembling.

"I have to go! Please leave," I said and went inside the house to get Mirta.

Still shaken by the kiss, I found Mirta in the dining room. She was engaged in an animated conversation with the rest of her family. I looked at her with fear in my eyes but didn't say anything.

Her mother said hello and asked me to join the others in the long dining room, but I stood there, staring at Mirta.

"You want to go back home?" Mirta asked.

I nodded. As if noticing my expression, she laughed and told her family she would be right back.

"What were you doing outside?" her mother asked.

"Mom, you know how shy Madeline is. Besides, she wasn't feeling too well and needed some fresh air."

Mirta's mother pressed her lips and gave her daughter an incredulous look.

By the time Mirta and I stepped on the porch, Willy had left.

"What happened?" Mirta said as we walked on the dirt road, lifting dust with our shoes.

"I'm so nervous. Oh my God! What happens if my mother finds out, or even worse, my father?"

"What did he do?"

"He kissed me!"

She laughed.

"Your first kiss! Oh my God! Well... did you like it?"

I said I didn't want to talk about it. She laughed again, as if knowing exactly what I meant.

"Yes, you liked it! I know you too well."

Afraid she would laugh at me about my reaction to a kiss on the cheek, I didn't clarify where he had kissed me.

After I told her about my refusal to let him speak to my father, she began to think about ways he and I could meet again without my parents' knowledge.

Chapter 7 – Mr. Avellaneda

Narrator: Madeline

"I'm so excited! My son is coming to spend New Year's Eve with me," Ana Cañizares, owner of the hair salon and ex-wife of a high-ranking government official, said as she removed my rollers.

It was the first week of December, three months after my fifteenth birthday.

"He's looking for a wife, you know?" she added while combing my hair and looking at our reflections in the mirror. "He wants to marry a nice girl, like you. God knows there aren't too many to choose from in this small town."

I listened for a moment, but then my mind drifted. I could see her moving her mouth in an endless monologue I could no longer hear. I'd travel to Mirta's porch, to the night Willy kissed me. While enveloped in my thoughts, I felt her touch on my shoulder.

"Did you hear my question?"

"I'm sorry," I said. "Do you mind repeating it?"

Chapter 7 – Mr. Avellaneda

"Never mind. I just know that if you see my son, you will fall in love with him. He has changed so much. He's a looker, you know?"

She finished styling my hair, and before I left, she kissed me on the cheek.

"Maybe we'll stop by your house this weekend," she said. "It's been a while since I've visited your mom."

I smiled, paid for her services, and left with my aunt Rita, who was spending time with me that afternoon and waited for me in the sitting area.

Two days later, voices coming from outside the house interrupted my reading. I rose from the living room's rocking chair and looked beyond the open front door, past the porch. I noticed a familiar face accompanied by someone I didn't know.

Wearing a white muslin-fabric dress with short sleeves and a puffy skirt, I rushed to the porch to greet Ana and the young man who accompanied her.

She introduced me to the tall, well-dressed young man. I extended my hand to him, and he brought it to his lips, while looking at me with an uncomfortable intensity.

"It's a pleasure to meet you, Madeline. My mother is always talking about you, and I can see why."

After giving him a polite smile, I retrieved my hand. I thought about what his mother had said at the salon. He was indeed attractive but not my type.

Chapter 7 – Mr. Avellaneda

"Please come in and make yourselves comfortable. I will call my mother."

Mother and son entered our living room and sat in the rocking chairs, while I went to the kitchen to announce the visitors.

Later, as Mamá and Ana exchanged pleasantries in the living room, at Ana's suggestion, her son and I went out to the porch. I kept the front door open and sat in a rocking chair my mother could see from inside.

Miguel Avellaneda explained how he had arrived from Havana the day before. He told me he planned to be in Arroyo Blanco for the holidays and then return to the capital. He wanted to follow in his father's footsteps and join Batista's military forces.

"I want to give my future wife a good life. With my father's position, it won't be difficult to move up through the ranks."

I didn't say anything. Marriage was the last thing in my mind, but he kept staring at me.

"Do you have a boyfriend?" he asked.

I smiled, unable to tell him the truth.

"No, Mr. Avellaneda. I don't have a boyfriend."

"I'm surprised," he said. "You're one of the most beautiful young women I've ever seen."

"Thank you for your kind words. It's just that my father is very strict. I spend most of my time here at home, reading."

"What do you like to read?"

"Romantic stories, mostly. Do *you* like to read?"

"I do, but I prefer books about history, politics, and the military."

Boring, I thought after his response and replied: "I don't like politics or anything dealing with the military."

"Well, I understand. After all, the role of a woman is to be a wife and a good mother and to let her husband worry about those types of issues."

I didn't respond. Although my parents had explained the different roles of men and women—men as providers and women as housekeepers and mothers—his words bothered me, and I couldn't wait for the visit to end. At a point during our conversation, I found myself thinking about Willy and about the kiss that swept me off my feet.

I tried to hide my relieved expression when my mother interrupted our conversation and handed each of us a small cup of steaming coffee. We drank it and returned empty cups to my mother.

"Delicious," he said. "Nothing compares to the coffee of Arroyo Blanco."

The caffeine made it easier to focus on our conversation, which had now shifted to his life in Havana. I had not been there before, and I couldn't imagine living in a place where people lived so close to each other, a place where roosters didn't wake me in the morning, or where mango trees didn't grow in my backyard.

Chapter 7 – Mr. Avellaneda

He told me about his intentions of marrying a girl from Arroyo Blanco.

"Any reason in particular, Mr. Avellaneda?"

"The farms are good for the spirit. They purify the soul."

"Are you saying the girls in Havana are not as pure?"

He smiled.

"I'm not saying that. They are different, a difference I can't describe but I can sense."

I raised my eyebrows.

"I don't think I understand you, Mr. Avellaneda, but I hope you find what you are looking for one day."

We remained silent for a moment. I turned my head towards the front yard, wishing I could see Willy driving his Jeep.

"Are you going to the New Year's party at the club?" he asked.

"We go every year."

"I'll be there. I would love it if you danced with me."

I noticed the glow of enthusiasm in his eyes.

"I'm not much of a dancer. My friend Mirta has shown me a few steps, but my mother doesn't like to see me dancing."

"Do you want me to talk to her?"

"No. That's not necessary. I'd rather keep things as they are."

He nodded.

"As you wish, but I will not give up so easily."

The visit didn't last much longer. However, after Mr. Avellaneda and his mother left, Mamá didn't waste time.

"Mr. Avellaneda seems like a very nice young man and from a good family," she said.

I shrugged.

"Don't you like him?"

"He wants a wife, and I'm not ready to be anyone's wife. I'm only fifteen."

"There are many girls your age who are already married. It's not unusual in the country, you know. Men like Mr. Avellaneda are hard to find. His father is very well connected."

"I'm not interested, Mamá. Can we talk about something else?"

"His mother asked me if her son could dance with you on New Year's Eve, and I said yes. Make sure you look beautiful that night and treat him with the kindness and respect he deserves."

"Didn't you say that decent girls don't dance?"

"Madeline, stop misinterpreting everything I say. This is different. I'll get with Adela. She needs to finish your outfit for the party right away. Give that young man a chance!"

I didn't respond. As always, I kept my thoughts inside, afraid of her pinches and her screams.

Adela, the seamstress my mother hired to make dresses for Nancy and me, had seen me grow up. In her late twenties, she had a round face and black hair she tied in a bun. Her mother, also a seamstress, had died when she was fifteen. She had taught her daughter all she knew about sewing, which allowed Adela to take over her mother's customers.

Adela treated me as a younger sister. When Mirta told her that I needed a way for Willy and me to exchange letters, she offered to be the carrier.

Mirta didn't want to cross my mother. I think she feared her. Also, Willy and I could not meet at Mirta's house any longer. Her mother befriended mine, and she had seen Willy and me talking the night of the birthday celebration. She reprimanded her daughter for facilitating our meeting and swore to tell my mother if it happened again.

Each time Adela brought me a letter from Willy, I hid in my room to read it. I enjoyed them as much as I enjoyed my Corín Tellado novels, and with each one, I grew more restless. In his letters, he professed his love for me, the way I kept him up at night. The way he described his family, so big and united, made me want to be part of it.

In one of his letters, after Willy heard from Mirta about my encounter with Mr. Avellaneda, he threatened to crash the New Year's celebration at the club. I assured him he had nothing to worry about and begged him to stay away.

Chapter 8 – New Year's Party

Narrator: Madeline

As the year 1955 neared its end, the preparations at the clubhouse were in full swing. While I worried about my hair and party attire, the seeds of the revolution germinated quickly, within Cuba and abroad. 1956 would bring about changes that would accelerate the pace of revolutionary efforts.

I was a teenager, oblivious to politics, and in many ways oblivious to life. So, there I was, on the day of the New Year's party, standing in front of the mirror. When Nancy entered the room, she placed her hands on her mouth in awe. She ran to me and embraced my legs.

"You look so pretty!" she said.

I was wearing a black velvet blouse with long sleeves, encrusted with several rows of rhinestones in the front. My taffeta skirt, black with decorative silver lines, had layers of stiffened petticoats underneath and was cinched in around my waist, reaching just below my knees.

Another year was ending, and I was happy. I wanted to grow up and leave my mother's firm grip. It suffocated me, but I realized that when the day to leave home arrived, I would miss my father and my sister the most. My father drove us to the party. We looked like the perfect family when we entered the club, my father in his stylish güayabera shirt, and the rest of us with our custom-made dresses and impeccable hairdos. The music played while the conversations, dancing, and wine enlivened the night.

It didn't take long for Mr. Avellaneda to spot me and join us. After exchanging pleasantries with my parents, he asked them for their permission to dance with me.

"Thank you. I don't dance," I said.

"I saw you dance in front of the mirror the other day," said Nancy in an innocent voice.

"Go dance with Mr. Avellaneda," my mother suggested.

"You take good care of my daughter," my father said.

I looked at my parents with pleading eyes. At that moment, Mr. Avellaneda grabbed my hand.

"Miss, could I have this dance?"

I allowed him to escort me to the dance floor, while the song "Bonito y Sabroso" by Benny Moré played in the background.

After leaving my sister with one of my aunts, my parents joined us on the dance floor. Having them near me made me feel better.

During our first dance, Mr. Avellaneda did most of the talking, asking me questions about the type of music I liked and talking about his plans. To be polite, I smiled occasionally, all along worrying about my boyfriend, wondering what would happen if he came to the party and saw me dancing with Mr. Avellaneda.

As the evening progressed, we alternated between dances and short conversation breaks, until midnight when everyone brought in the New Year with a toast. At the end of the evening, he asked me if he could speak to my parents about becoming my boyfriend.

"Mr. Avellaneda, I'm not interested in you in that manner. There is someone else who has my heart, and when the appropriate time comes, *he* will speak to my father."

He looked at me with confusion.

"I thought you liked me," he said.

"As a friend, yes, I do. You're a good man, and I'm convinced you'll find the right girl one day, but that's not me. I think you have misinterpreted my kindness."

Judging by the disappointment in his eyes, I realized I had ruined his night.

"I'm sorry, miss. If you ever change your mind, I would appreciate it if you gave me a chance."

"I will keep that in mind. Good night."

He escorted me to where my parents were standing and explained that an unforeseen event had occurred requiring his attention.

That was the last time I saw him.

Mirta later told me that when Willy heard that Mr. Avellaneda had danced with me at the party, he talked to him to make sure it didn't happen again. Without knowing, Willy put the fear of God into him. Not that he was a violent man, but everyone knew about his eight brothers, who were not only close to one another, but who would do anything if any harm, real or perceived, came to the family.

Chapter 9 – The Visit

Narrator: Willy

The annual fair arrived at the baseball stadium like it did every year, during the month of July, close to the celebration of the Carnival of San Juan—when the stadium was dressed in vibrant colors and laughter for two weeks.

It was a busy time at the Port of Guayabal located over 40 kilometers away. With so much work at the port, my father, my male siblings, and I didn't have enough time to care for the livestock.

Despite my busy schedule, I needed to make time for the girl with whom I had fallen in love. We had been dating for several months through letters and casual encounters that always included her friend Mirta, but on this day, I was determined to speak to her alone.

I didn't know if my plan would work. In case it did, to impress her, I wore my best outfit, a pair of translucent dark-blue pants and a long-sleeve white shirt.

Chapter 9 – The Visit

The town had come alive as an organ grinder played popular music by turning a handle on a street organ connected to loudspeakers. After one of the songs finished, he announced with a suave voice: "And now, '*Angustia*' for the *angustiados*." He began to play a popular romantic song about anguish and longing, a favorite of Madeline's, according to her letters.

People stood in line to ride the carousel, the Ferris wheel, and the chair swings, among a dozen other rides.

While '*Angustia*' was playing, I searched for Madeline, anxious, desperate to see her. A couple of my friends passed by and said hello. I didn't want to appear rude, but I kept the conversations brief. They seemed surprised.

"I'm in a hurry. I'll talk to you tomorrow," I said.

I continued to scan the crowd until my face lit up when I saw her. There she was, standing in line by the Ferris wheel, accompanied by her friends. I didn't see her parents and assumed they were at another ride. As usual, Mirta stood by her side, talking to her about something that caused Madeline to laugh. I came closer to them, trying to get Mirta's attention, watching Madeline, as beautiful as ever, under the glow of colorful lights. For a moment, Mirta turned her head towards me. With a wave of my hand, I asked her to follow me. She did, and we spoke behind the popcorn stand.

Chapter 9 – The Visit

"Please help me," I said. "I need to talk to her alone."

Judging by the way she laughed, my desperation seemed to amuse her.

"Don't worry. I'll see what I can do."

When she rejoined the group, she whispered something in Madeline's ear as I stood a few meters away. Madeline and I then exchanged glances.

When it was Madeline's turn to ride, Mirta signaled at me and asked me to her place in line. When I went on the ride with Madeline, the other girls chuckled. Minutes later, Madeline and I found ourselves alone above the crowd. We looked down and watched as families played games of chance at the bazaars and bought popcorn, cotton candy, or sodas.

Madeline glanced at me for a moment and then evaded my eyes. I reached for her hand and held it within mine. It was ice cold.

"I missed you," I said.

"Me too."

As I framed her face with my hands and kissed her cheek, she burst into tears.

"What's wrong Madi? Why are you crying?"

"This won't work."

"Why?"

"My parents will never allow it. I can't talk to Mamá. I'm afraid of her. I don't know what to do."

"Madi, my angel," I said caressing her hands. "Everything will be fine. I'll take care of everything. You need to be patient, like I am. I will wait as long as it takes."

She took her handkerchief from her purse and wiped her tears. She smelled like jasmine, an aroma that stayed with me long after that night.

"I will talk to your father."

"You have to wait. Dad is not ready."

"He has to understand how much we love each other. I can't stand to see you cry."

"Please wait."

I insisted, but when she didn't change her mind, I switched the topic and began to ask her questions about herself, her likes and dislikes. I could see her growing more comfortable as she spoke, until I no longer had to ask questions because she started a monologue about her sister and her parents. I could have listened to her forever. After she finished, I told her a few jokes. She laughed, even at the bad ones.

Our conversation reinforced my determination not to allow anyone to get in our way.

The next day, after lunch, I told my father about my plans. He looked at me but didn't say anything and walked away. Moments later, as I was getting the Jeep ready, I heard my mother's voice.

"Your father just told me what you are about to do. Have you lost your mind?"

"Why you say that, *mi vieja*?"

"You don't know how her father will react. Everyone knows he has a gun. What if he does something to you? Please stay. With all the pretty girls in town, you have to choose her?"

I smiled and kissed her on the cheek.

"I love you, Vieja. Don't worry about me. I'll be fine."

I sat on the driver's seat and closed the door, while she looked at me with pleading eyes.

"I beg you."

"See you later. Don't worry."

I left her standing by the side of the house and drove away.

Thinking I would not dare to confront her father, Madeline had not alerted him, so my visit surprised her as much as it surprised him.

To try to impress her father, I wore the same pants from the night before and a white long-sleeve shirt.

Madeline was sitting on the porch reading when I parked in front of her house. The moment she saw me, she ran inside without saying a word.

The door stayed wide open as I stepped on the porch.

"Hello," I said and waited by the front door.

Moments later, her father came out buttoning his shirt.

"Good afternoon," he said with inquisitive eyes.

"Good afternoon, Mr. Rodriguez. I'm sorry to bother you. My name is Willy Montes, and I'm here to speak to you about your daughter."

"What business could you have with my daughter?" he asked with a stern tone of voice, looking down at me.

"I would like to visit her, sir," I said.

His eyes widened in astonishment.

"*My* daughter?"

"Madeline, sir. I'm in love with her. I want to assure you I have good intentions. As the decent girl that she is, I would not want to see her outside your house. The last thing I want is to disrespect you or her, sir."

"*My* daughter? Do you realize she's only a girl?"

"She loves me and agreed to be my girl-friend, sir."

Mr. Rodriguez began to speak with his hands.

"My daughter doesn't know what she wants, and neither do you!" He paused for a moment, took a step towards me, and pointed at my face. "Get out! If you know what's good for you, don't you ever put a foot anywhere near this house! You hear me?"

"I'll leave, sir. This is your house, and I owe you my respect, but nothing will change how I feel about Madeline."

"Get out!"

I never anticipated Mr. Rodriguez's reaction, nor did I understand why Madeline had run away.

Chapter 9 – The Visit

Later I heard from Mirta that Mr. Rodriguez didn't say much to his daughter about my visit, other than:

"Don't worry. I'll take care of it."

Her mother, on the other hand, spent the rest of the afternoon screaming, her arms over her head, as if the world were coming to end.

Following my meeting with her father, I didn't see Madeline for several days. I learned from Mirta that Madeline's parents had sent her to her grandparents' house to get her away from me.

Her grandfather was a wealthy landowner who had extensive fields of guava, sugarcane, coconut, potatoes, and anything that could grow his fertile soil. Castro and his rebels called people like him *latifundistas*. He represented the type of person his revolution opposed, perhaps because of jealousy, or because he thought those who had achieved that level of wealth had stolen it from others.

I knew that wasn't true. Madeline's grandfather, according to Mirta, had worked like a horse during his younger years, saving every *peso* to purchase more and more parcels of land. He made sound investment decisions that paid off over time. Nothing was given to him.

He and his family lived on a large farm of 150 *caballerías* located several kilometers away from Arroyo Blanco, a journey of over forty minutes by Jeep via a dirt road.

It didn't matter to me how far her parents had taken her. All I knew was that nothing her

Chapter 9 – The Visit

parents could do would take me away from the woman I loved.

Chapter 10 – Sent Away

Narrator: Madeline

The moment I arrived at my paternal grandparents' farmhouse, I dashed past the living room towards my bedroom and didn't say hello to anyone. I threw myself on the bed and lay there, staring at the tall ceiling, noticing the elaborate crown moldings. The beige wall paint contrasted against the white molding, appearing more beautiful than I remembered. A soft breeze slipped in through the open windows, and I could hear a tractor and the voices of farm workers.

I got up and cracked open the door a bit to listen in on my parents' conversation. They and my sister had stayed with my grandmother in the living room, only a few meters away from my bedroom.

"I can't believe she's treating us like this after all you have done for her, Victorino," my mother said. "You don't deserve this and neither do I. Why does she have to pick a nobody? There are so many eligible men in town." I could feel the blood rushing to my face. Then I heard my father's voice.

"Esperanza, stop!"

Chapter 10 – Sent Away

"It's the truth!"

"This conversation is over," my father replied. He paused for a moment before he directed his attention to his mother. "Well, Mamá, I have a lot to do. I need to drive back. Give my father a hug for me."

"You're going to leave without eating? Let me get the chef to prepare you something."

"Thank you, but I can't stay."

I heard the movement of furniture.

"Let's go, Nancy. Pick up your toys," my mother said.

"Can I give my big sister a hug before we go?"

Mamá's response didn't surprise me.

"Your sister is not setting a good example for you. Let's just go home. You'll see her next time."

I heard the decreasing sound of footsteps and then silence.

I jumped back on my bed, put a pillow over my head, and crossed my arms. After a while, my grandmother Matilde came into my room dragging her feet, sat on the edge of bed, and removed the pillow off my face.

"No hugs for your grandmother?"

I didn't respond.

"Your father told me what happened. Give him time, my love. You're still his little girl, you know?"

She placed her arthritic hands on my arm and took a deep breath.

"Let me know if you need anything. We can talk when you're ready."

I glanced at her for a moment. She must have been in her sixties, but her wrinkles made her look older. Her eyeglasses distorted the amber in her eyes and revealed her good nature. Yet I couldn't let my guard down and focused once again on the ceiling. Part of me wanted to hug her. I couldn't get myself to do it, too worried about my feelings to realize how my behavior affected her.

She stayed by my side for a while. After she left, I began to weep out of frustration. I didn't recognize myself. I had always enjoyed the time I spent at my grandparents' house. Not during this visit. I felt tired, as if nothing mattered.

My grandparents, Maximino and Matilde, personified kindness and love. Married over fifty years, they had raised five boys and six girls. Grandpa managed the farm and a store where his workers purchased food for their families. My grandmother controlled everything else.

My father had inherited Grandma's leadership skills. She sat at the head of the dining room table and gave orders to the workers. She had maids who kept the house clean, a chef who prepared tasty meals, and house workers who went on errands for her. The workers seemed as dedicated and loyal to her as she was to them.

"You didn't get enough salad and meat," she would tell them as we all sat around the long dining room table.

Her one-eyed chef had worked for her for years. He cooked flavorful beef, chicken, or pork with potatoes and delicious fried pork. He also prepared avocado and tomato salad, all vegetables and meat cultivated or raised on their farm.

My grandmother liked order and discipline. The house workers and our family had to eat at a specific time. The only workers who didn't sit at our table were those who worked on the farm. They lived in small houses provided by my grandfather, and their families cooked their meals.

Later that day, my grandmother returned to my room and asked me to join everyone at the table for dinner. I complied. There must have been over a dozen people around the table, most of them aunts, uncles, and their families. I ate little, feeling out of place for the first time. After a while, I asked to be excused and returned to my bed.

When the night arrived, I could hear the noise in the house die down as my relatives returned to their houses and my grandparents and house workers went to bed. I couldn't sleep. Thinking that looking at the fields would help me relax, I looked out my window. It was then I saw my grandmother's silhouette. She hid behind a tall oak tree, smoking a cigarette under the moonlight. I recalled that my father and his siblings had ordered house and farm workers not to bring her cigarettes because she suffered from emphysema, but my grandmother had a strong personality. Perhaps some of that spirit of contradiction lived within me. I had hidden well for years until Willy came into my life.

The day after my arrival at my grandparents' house, Aunt Rosita, my favorite aunt, came to stay with her parents for a few days. When she heard what happened, she came into my room and asked me to follow her to the porch.

We sat on angled rocking chairs facing each other.

"Tell me about this boy," she said.

"I love him, Tía Rosita," I said. "He is all I think about. Please help us. Papá doesn't understand."

She held my hands within hers.

"Don't worry. This will be resolved soon. Be patient."

I remained silent, noticing the pretty pink dress she wore that day. She didn't look like my grandmother who had a chubby and short body. Rosita was tall and slim with beautiful black hair and creamy-white skin.

"Would you like a tall glass of coconut juice and a couple of guavas?" Rosita asked.

I shrugged. She smiled and called one of our farm workers. I saw him climbing two of the trees, then I turned my attention to my aunt. A few minutes later, one of the maids brought me a tall glass of fresh coconut water and a plate with thick slices of peeled guavas and cream cheese.

My ability to ask for anything I wanted and having a worker fulfill my wish made me feel guilty sometimes. Rosita explained that if we didn't give a job to those workers, they would not be able to provide for their families. Her explanation didn't make me feel any better.

At first, I wondered why Rosita had come to the farm alone. She explained that her husband was traveling on business, and she wanted to spend some time with me.

During the long lazy afternoons, when Aunt Rosita and I sat in rocking chairs on Grandpa's wrap-around porch, I talked to her about Willy.

"I dream about him all the time. Not being able to see him hurts me. Papá thinks that keeping me away will change how I feel. I won't, Tía Rosita. I love Papá, and I don't want to have to choose between him and Willy."

"You have been bitten by the love bug, my child. Only those who have known love understand how you feel."

Chapter 11 – At Last

Narrator: Madeline

"Madi will be vacationing with her grand-parents for a few weeks," my mother told Mirta when she came to my house to see me a couple of days after I left.

Lying didn't come easily to my mother. Her expression always gave her away, and in this case, her words did too. "Don't tell *that man* where she is."

Mirta immediately suspected what was going on and ignored her request. That same day, she visited Willy and told him what had happened.

A few days later, when Aunt Rosita and I sat on the porch talking about Willy, I heard a loud engine noise. I looked up in the distance, and beyond the barbed wire fence, I saw his green Jeep with the top down. He waved at me several times, and I waved back.

"Who's that?" Tía Rosita asked.

"It's him."

"Aww... How romantic! He drove all the way here to see you. He must be in love."

We followed him with our eyes as he drove by a couple of times. His Jeep then stopped by the portion of the fence closest to us. He stood on the driver's seat and waved at me with more impetus than before. He also threw me kisses. I waved back, happy to see him. Then, noticing that Tía Rosita was waving at him too, I gave her a hug.

Out of respect for my grandparents, that's all Willy did that day. After he left, Tía Rosita noticed my gloomy eyes and longing expression.

"You love that man, don't you?" she asked.

I looked at her, not like the little girl she had seen grow before her eyes, but like a woman.

"I do, Tía Rosita. My heart beats faster when I see him. When he's not near me, I feel broken."

Believing love doesn't knock on one's door often, and when it does, one must answer, she realized she had to speak to my grandfather.

"Dad, Madi is in love," she told him. "She's no longer a child. The more my brother opposes this relationship, the worse it will be. She may even run away," she exaggerated, like she often did.

My grandfather asked my uncles to begin a formal investigation. They spoke to everyone who knew Willy and his family. They also visited his parents. After my uncles returned with their recommendation, my grandfather met with my father. He told him that Willy came from a hard-working family and was a good man.

One day, Papá came to my grandparents' house alone and told me he was taking me home. Eight weeks had passed since my departure.

"I don't want any harm to come to you," he told me as we were driving away. "I hope you know that. When I do things, I do them thinking of your best interest."

My eyes filled with tears.

"I know, Papá."

"Do you love that man?" he asked.

I nodded, and he took a deep breath.

"Get a message to him and tell him to meet with me at our house. I will talk to him."

I burst into sobs. Papá took his hand off the steering wheel for a moment and tapped me on the shoulder.

The next day, I talked to Mirta, and she arranged the meeting. That weekend, I waited for Willy on the porch. Anxious, I began to read a new book that my father had given me for my birthday.

When I heard the engine and saw his green Jeep in the distance, I closed the book and placed it on a table. A couple of minutes later, he parked in front of the house. I rose from the rocking chair and leaned over the veranda railing to invite him in.

"I'm sorry, but I won't go in," he said.

"But why?"

"Your father kicked me out of his house, and he has to invite me back in."

I shook my head.

"Fine, I'll go get him."

I rushed to the back of the house and told my father what Willy had said. He seemed pleased.

He accompanied me to the porch, but not before telling my little sister to stay in her room playing. He greeted Willy as he would a business colleague, with a firm handshake and a "please come in and have a seat."

They sat next to each other on the rocking chairs, while my mother and I sat across from them. Mamá looked at Willy with distrust and me with disappointment, discarding the illusions of a fifteen-year-old who was in love with love.

I looked towards the back of the house and saw my sister tiptoeing closer to the living room. I shifted my eyes in her direction without moving my head and opened them wide. She returned to her bedroom, only to return minutes later.

"What are your intentions with my daughter?" my father asked Willy.

"I love her, sir," Willy replied, looking him in the eye. "And if you allow me, I would like to marry her."

It was the first time I had heard the word marriage, and I felt scared and excited at the same time. Upon hearing that word, my mother stared at me with an angry expression and crossed her arms.

"First things first, son," my father said, repositioning himself into his seat. "If you want to marry her, you must be willing to wait until she turns eighteen. In the meantime, you have my permission to visit her. However, you must treat her as the decent girl that she is. Do we understand each other?"

"Yes, sir. This is a small sacrifice. I will wait as long as I have to."

"I still don't understand why you couldn't find a woman your own age. She's a child."

"We love each other, sir. I just turned twenty. I'm only five years older than she is."

"Five years make a big difference."

"I know you can't read inside my mind, and it's hard for you to trust me when you don't really know me. I hope that years from now, you will realize that this was the right thing to do. I love her with all my being."

Willy and I exchanged glances. I smiled at him, but when my mother noticed it, she gave me a discrete slap on my hand that wiped the smile off my face.

"I'm sorry about how I've treated you. I thought that Madeline was still a child. I now see she's no longer my little girl. She's a young woman."

My father looked at me with admiration shrouded in sadness. At that moment, I wanted to tell him that my heart had enough love for him and Willy. That would never change. I hoped the loving glance I gave him at that moment conveyed that message.

Willy began to visit our house, at first under the strict schedule my father dictated.

Chapter 11 – At Last

Every Sunday, I wore my best dress and waited for him on the porch. For the first few weeks, we sat outside and talked with the playfulness of children. Mamá always offered him coffee, out of politeness, not because she liked him. My father gave her the role of chaperone while he stayed in the bedroom reading. When my mother returned the empty cups to the kitchen, Willy and I would hold hands, but I sensed he longed for something more.

By the third visit, when Mamá went for coffee, he leaned towards me, and his lips met mine for the first time. They enveloped them with desperation, revealing a softness and warmth that sent tingles through my body. I closed my eyes and surrendered my mouth to his. I enjoyed the way he made me feel, the way he elevated me to the heavens. I didn't know how long that first kiss lasted, or what made me return to reality, perhaps the thought that my mother would be back at any moment.

"She'll see us," I said after freeing my lips.

We both leaned back into our seats, and I wiped my mouth with my fingers. As I glanced at him, I noticed my lipstick smeared on his face.

"Wipe your face!"

"What?"

"Hurry! You have lipstick..."

He brought his hands to his mouth and wiped his lips clean. Not even a minute later, my mother arrived with two cups of coffee. We drank the liquid without looking at each other, and after she returned inside with the empty cups, we burst into laughter.

After the sixth visit, my father took us, my mother, and my sister to my grandfather's farm where a big family feast awaited. That was the first of many.

It didn't take long for Willy to gain the affection of Tía Rosita and my grandparents.

Five months after Willy's first visit, he brought me a pretty gold band with five diamonds and asked me to be his wife. I accepted.

To celebrate our engagement, his family organized a party in the coastal town of Guayabal, the place where he was building us a house. He didn't want to work on the farm anymore and found Guayabal to be an affordable option with access to a good job. On the day of the celebration, we drove there in two Jeeps, Willy's parents and a couple of his brothers in one, and Willy, Nancy, my parents, and I in another.

Driving on an elevated gravel road, surrounded by farms and forests, it took us over an hour to get there. All along, my anticipation grew as Willy insisted on concealing any details of the party.

I could now smell the aromatic sea-air as we drove down the road with our windows down and the Jeep's top removed. Nothing I would have imagined could compare to what happened next. Approaching the end of the road, we turned onto a long sandy street paralleling the beach lined with tiny houses on either side. Suddenly, a crowd of people, perhaps hundreds, burst into cheers. As we stepped out of the vehicle, smiles and handshakes welcomed us with congratulations for our engagement and comments like "she is so pretty," and "we wish you many happy years." My parents looked around in awe, Mamá with a shy smile and my father trying to hide his discomfort. I didn't know how Willy managed to do it, but on that day, he made me feel like a queen.

We visited some of the houses in the quaint town. On our first stop, one of Willy's aunts served us a lunch typical of the area: white rice, dried shrimp, and *boniato*. The shrimp, dried under the sun, was considered a delicacy. During our next stop, we ate fresh snapper, and in the last one, we enjoyed homemade guava shells in a thick syrup, served with cream cheese. We met over a dozen relatives at each house, including many aunts, uncles, and cousins.

During each visit, I glanced at my father, trying to read his thoughts, hoping he could feel joy in my happiness.

We returned home a couple of hours before sunset, exhausted, but the memories of that trip would always stay with me.

***

The years after our engagement went by quickly between family life and the visits to my maternal grandmother's house and my paternal grandparents' farm.

During those happy times, when we sat around a long dining room table, conversing with our extended family members and eating delicious black beans and rice with fresh pork and plantains, or meat and potatoes, or the most delectable yellow rice and chicken with luscious red peppers, I could not have foreseen how much the love Willy and I had for each other would be tested.

Chapter 12 – The Rebels

Narrator: Madeline

Knocking sounds and loud voices awoke me in the middle of the night.

"Open up! Open the door right now, or we'll burn down the house!" a man said.

From the bedroom my sister and I shared, I heard my mother screaming. Half-asleep, Nancy turned to the other side and placed the sheet over her head.

"Nancy, wake up! Hurry!"

"I'm tired. Leave me alone!"

"Nancy, it's not safe to stay here. Let's go!"

Reluctantly, she got up.

"There's a bad man outside the house," I whispered. "Don't say a word."

I grabbed my sister's hand, and we rushed to our parents' bedroom. By the time we got there, my mother was inconsolable.

"What's going on?" I asked.

Papá gave us a hug.

"Girls, stay here with your mother and don't leave this room unless I say so."

He then grabbed a shirt he had left on top of a chair and put it on.

"What are you doing?" Mamá asked him.

"What I have to," he said in a calm way as he buttoned his shirt.

I placed my arms around Nancy and caressed her hair while I glanced at my father to ascertain if he shared my fright. However, the moonlight filtering through the windows didn't illuminate the room enough for me to read his face.

"You're running out of time!" a male voice said. It was a cold and unsympathetic voice, the type one doesn't ever forget. Then deafening metal-banging noises followed. Terrified, I started to breathe faster and held Nancy closer to me.

"You hear that?" the man yelled. "These are gasoline tanks. We're getting them ready now."

"I'm scared," said Nancy placing her little arms around me.

"Don't be," I said. "Everything will be okay."

I caressed her hair and looked in my parents' direction. My mother rushed to my father as he tried to leave the room, grabbed him by his shirt, and shook him while yelling in her typical dramatic fashion, "don't let them kill us, Victorino!" She then broke into sobs.

My father freed himself from her grasp. Then, as if he had forgotten to do something, he rushed towards one of the windows. He pushed the thin curtains aside and peered out, repeating these steps on the opposite side of the room.

"The house is surrounded by trucks and armed men," he said to my mother. "Stay here until I return."

Between sobs, she kept begging him not to go, and when he insisted, she said, "Please return to us."

After my father exited the room, Mamá joined Nancy and me in the corner of the room and grabbed our hands.

"God, help our family. Please don't let anything happen to my husband and my girls."

She closed her eyes, held us in a tight embrace, and whispered more prayers.

We heard the diminishing sound of my father's footsteps and listened to the squeaking noise of hinges.

"Give me any weapons you have in the house and all the bullets. Also, bring me the keys to that Jeep. It'll come handy. And don't try anything because I won't hesitate for one second to put a bullet in you, and then I'll burn down your house with your family in it. Trust me. They won't be able to escape."

The man sounded serious. My father told him he didn't have to worry. He would comply. Moments later, Dad walked into the room and retrieved his gun and the bullets from the dresser drawer.

"What are you doing?" my mother asked.

"Protecting my family. These are dangerous men. They're rebels."

"Please be careful," Mamá replied.

Chapter 12 – The Rebels

My father left the room again. After that, time moved at a very slow pace. I feared for his life. I hoped he would not do anything to anger the rebels. We all stayed very quiet, even Mamá who took deep breaths to drown the sound of her emotions. Then, we listened. We heard my father's voice but could not decipher what he said. Then, we heard a door close and the sound of the trucks driving away.

That was my first encounter with Castro's revolutionaries. It was the start of the year 1958. Things would only get worse. After the men left, my father returned to the room.

"They'll pay for what they did!" he said, clenching his jaw and hitting the dresser with his closed fists.

My mother, my sister, and I surrounded him with our embraces while I could hear him breathing faster, as if he had been running. Weeping, my mother placed her hand on his chest for a moment and told him that his heart was beating as hard as a drum. I had never seen him that angry.

By dawn, our house was full of people, from the authorities to my father's bosses, all trying to reassure my father they would protect us, none of them realizing that irreversible damage had been done to our country and that anyone's ability to protect those who opposed the rebels had vanished.

Once everyone left, the house turned quiet again. Mamá returned to her chores, and Papá began to pace around the house, buried in thought. His bosses had given him the day off.

By noon, I was in the living room trying to concentrate on a Corín Tellado novel when a galloping sound distracted me. I looked out through the window. In the distance, I saw Willy and his horse, and I rushed outside.

I would later learn from one of his sisters that as soon as he heard the news, he began to act irrationally, telling his brothers and sisters what he was going to do to the rebels if they placed a finger on me. He was so angry that his brothers had to restrain him while his mother went to the house and brought him a glass of water and a cup of linden leaf tea to help him calm down. Before he left the farm, his brothers asked him to take the horse, afraid the rebels would take the Jeep.

Willy looked preoccupied as he dismounted his horse and secured it near the house. Moments later, we embraced, and I cried in his arms as my father watched us from inside.

It was nine months before my eighteenth birthday, and my town had lost its innocence. People in the area stayed in their homes after 6 p.m. because the woods were full of revolutionaries. Those who had to be out at that time were detained by the rebels and questioned, some killed.

The rebels injected fear into the fiber of every country town. One day, Roberto, one of Willy's neighbors, was lifting sugarcane off the fields with a crane when he was confronted by some of Batista's troops.

"Hey you! Have you seen any rebels around here?" one of the soldiers yelled.

"Of course," he said. "Everybody sees them, except for you."

Later that day, Roberto received a message from his brother to inform him that their father had had a stroke. Roberto gathered his three children and his wife and went to his father's house. That evening, a group of rebels surrounded his house and set it on fire. From his farm, about a kilometer away, Willy could see the glow of giant orange flames and the trail of smoke reaching for the sky. If Roberto's father had not suffered a stroke, Roberto would have been murdered with his entire family. It was apparent that one of Batista's soldiers had contacted the rebels regarding his response.

That same year, two other townsmen, accused of being snitches and disparaging the revolution, lost their lives at the hands of the rebels. Everyone in town knew about it. In the middle of the night, large groups of armed men, like those who visited my house, came to their homes and shot them dead in front of their families, increasing the environment of fear that reigned in our towns.

Chapter 13 – The Wedding

Narrator: Willy

"It's already dark, Madi. I should go," I said.

Madeline and I were standing on her front porch while her parents watched us from inside the house.

"Why don't you stay in the living room tonight? It's dangerous to be out there this late," she said, turning her head towards her parents, seeking approval.

"I have to get up very early."

"What if the rebels stop you?" she whispered.

"Don't worry. I'll be fine," I said, unsure of whether I had any chance against them.

I kissed Madeline on the cheek and said goodbye to her parents, then headed home.

I was tired. My lazy horse galloped at a slow pace on the dirt road. With the moonlight guiding me home, I kept dozing off. To stay awake, I shook my head several times and slapped my face.

At some point, I fell asleep, but my horse's sudden stop woke me. Disoriented, I tried to gain my balance as the scared animal attempted to buck me. What could have triggered this reaction?

I dismounted the horse, caressed his face, and talked to him in a soft, calm voice, but he seemed restless and nervous. I looked around, trying to figure out what had scared him. Then I saw a group of armed men sprinting from behind several buildings. I was surrounded by rebels.

"Who are you?" one of bearded men yelled.

"Willy Montes."

"What are you doing outside? Don't you know you shouldn't be out at this time? Are you a snitch?"

"I'm not. I left my girlfriend's house late, and I'm on my way home."

One of the rebels came from behind me and put a gun to my head.

"Either you tell me the truth, or I'll kill you, you son-of-a-bitch. What are you doing out at this hour?"

He came so close to me I could smell his foul breath. I tried to remain calm, but the thought that I would not make it home that evening crossed my mind.

"I went to see my girlfriend and lost track of time. If that's a crime, then I'm willing to die for the woman I love."

They all began to laugh. I could feel the barrel of the gun against my temple. If the man who held it pressed the trigger, all would end there. What would happen to Madeline then?

Chapter 13 – The Wedding

Who would protect her? It took everything I had to control my breathing and not let fear overcome me.

After a couple of tense minutes, one of the men gestured to another who walked up to me and said:

"Listen to me, Romeo. If we ever catch you outside this late, there won't be another chance."

The man with the gun returned it to his holster. Then I got back on my horse and galloped away.

After that encounter, I wondered if Madeline and I should move up the wedding. As time passed, I had to spend more time working at the Port of Guayabal, which didn't allow me the opportunity to visit her as often. The commute between the towns had become more dangerous, and I feared that soon, I would not be able to make the journey.

With the good money I was making, I had enough to finish the house, but I could not do it alone. I talked to my brothers, and they agreed to help me.

When the house was finished, I met with Madeline's father and asked him if I could marry her sooner. He was getting older, and after giving up his weapon, he didn't think he could keep his daughter safe. I, on the other hand, had my brothers and knew how to fight, not only in the boxing ring but on the street.

So, a new date was set, three weeks earlier than anticipated.

Chapter 13 – The Wedding

On November 23rd, I came to Madeline's house ready to marry her. We were in the middle of a war, so there would be no party or fancy ceremony. We borrowed a Jeep from the company where her father worked, and her father, Madeline, her sister, her mother, and I began the dangerous journey to visit the notary, who had a practice a few kilometers away in Santa Cruz del Sur. We were unaware of the conditions in that part of town when we left the house. Communications were limited, and there were only a couple of news programs on the radio during the day. The rest of the time, radio stations played music or soap operas.

We drove for a while on a dirt country road. Her father didn't say much along the way and had the face of someone who was going to a funeral, while Esperanza kept asking me questions about my parents and my brothers. After a while, we began to see a bridge in the distance, but something wasn't right. There was smoke everywhere, and before long, we started to see the rising flames on either side of the bridge. We concluded that the rebels had set it on fire. We had to drive through it to get to the other side in order to make it to our appointment on time, so instead of slowing down, Madeline's father pushed the accelerator. We were moving at a fast pace, and the Jeep kept bouncing from side to side over the uneven road.

"Get down on your seats!" Victorino yelled.

Chapter 13 – The Wedding

Nancy began to cry. She was sitting in the back seat between Madeline and me. We divided our attention between what was happening outside the Jeep and consoling Nancy. Madeline kept looking at me with fear in her eyes. Ahead, the Najasa River awaited, and we were approaching it quickly. Esperanza began to scream:

"What are you going to do?"

Victorino kept accelerating. "Keep your heads down! Madeline, cover your sister with your body. It may get rough ahead."

"Don't cross it, Dad! Stop the Jeep, please!" Madeline screamed.

"Take care of your sister!" he yelled.

Moments later, we were crossing the bridge at full speed. Thick smoke and fire surrounded us. Nancy and the women began to scream. I didn't admit it, but I was afraid our truck would go through the wooden bridge floor and plunge into the river. The next few minutes went by slowly while I kept thinking about what to do if the bridge collapsed, but moments later, we made it to the dirt road again and the screaming stopped.

Thirty minutes later, Madeline and I were standing in front of the local justice of the peace. It was a simple ceremony. No wedding dress or fancy suit, just two people professing eternal love to each other. Two of Victorino's friends who lived in that town served as our witnesses. By this time, as rebels continued to increase their span of control, people around these parts had stopped getting married at churches. Churches in this area now belonged to the past.

After we became husband and wife, the notary suggested a local restaurant where we could hold a quiet family gathering.

The restaurant was half full when we arrived. The chubby-faced woman at the entrance seemed glad to see us and, with a smile, led us to a long table. Throughout our meal, Victorino kept looking at his daughter, pressing his lips together and looking down when he thought no one was watching the tears in his eyes. Soon, he would have to say goodbye to his little girl. I hoped my reassuring glances conveyed what was in my heart. I had waited three years to marry the most beautiful girl of Arroyo Blanco. I loved her like I'd never loved anyone in my life, and I would not allow any harm to come to her. That was my promise, one that would be put through the test in unimaginable ways.

Chapter 14 – A New Life

Narrator: Madeline

Enrique, one of Willy's brothers, picked us up at my house upon our return from our wedding. "I'll come for my things in the morning, Papá," I told my father before I kissed him goodbye.

As we drove away, I started to become anxious. Sitting next to me in the back seat of the old Jeep, Willy asked me, "Are you happy?"

"Yes," I said, wondering if that had been my first lie. I feared being alone with him, not knowing how to be a wife.

The sun was setting on the horizon. Soon, the rebels would take over the area, so we spent the night at Enrique's house. This proved to be a blessing because that evening, we only cuddled and fell asleep in each other's arms. He wanted much more. Out of respect for his brother and his family, we waited.

The next morning his brother paid Julio, a man with close ties to the rebels, to pick us up. Julio was granted safe passage from a high ranking revolutionary and came for us in a

Chapter 14 – A New Life

large military truck. We gathered our belongings, said our goodbyes, and began our trip south through rebel-infested areas of the countryside.

Our truck was stopped several times along the way. I looked down each time, avoiding eye contact. I wore a simple grey dress, nothing that would cause the rebels to conclude that my father belonged to the social class they despised.

As the truck continued its steady progress, I glanced at the large Ceiba trees along the way and listened to the sound of parakeets and hummingbirds. Willy kept looking at me with happy eyes as he held and caressed my hand. His devouring glances made me think about what would happen in a few hours; our first night alone.

Guayabal awaited us with sunny skies. When we arrived at the tiny house Willy had built for us, the driver and two of Willy's brothers who had been riding in the back of the truck helped Willy bring our belongings inside.

I went to the kitchen with a small box that contained a coffee strainer and a colander, an iron pot, ground coffee, sugar, and metal cups. As I boiled water for the coffee, I began to organize the groceries, pots, pans, and kitchen utensils that Willy brought in.

Later, as I went outside with a tray holding several coffee cups, I held my breath. I had tasted a cup, but as a novice coffee maker, I didn't trust my judgement. When I saw them smile and return the empty cups, I wondered if they liked it or were making fun of me until Willy said, "Excellent coffee, *mi amor.*"

While the men arranged the furniture, I prepared ham and cheese sandwiches for them. I felt relieved when, at four-o-clock, the work ended, and everyone returned to their homes.

Willy and I finished organizing everything by seven. When we were done, he asked me to get ready for bed while he cooked me a steak and fries for dinner. As I showered, I wondered if I had already failed as a wife. My mother would have never allowed my father to cook for her.

He took a quick shower while I set the table. Then I sat and waited for him, while the aroma of crispy fries and fried steak, sautéed in onions, made me hungry.

Willy devoured his food in minutes, as if he hadn't eaten for days. My nervousness only allowed me to eat half of the food on my plate. After dinner, he asked me not to worry about the dishes.

As he took my hand and led me to the bedroom, my hands turned clammy.

"Don't worry," he said as if sensing my edginess.

When I saw him without a shirt for the first time, I was so impressed and scared by his muscles that I looked the other way.

"Are you afraid?" he asked.

I shrugged. I was standing by the bed, and he approached and began to kiss me, first on my cheeks, then my lips and neck. I trembled as he unbuttoned my dress.

"Don't worry," he said.

I felt tightness in my stomach. For the first time, he would be able to see my imperfections, and I felt ashamed.

"You're so much more beautiful than I had imagined," he said. I tried to cover myself with my hands and focus on something else, like the candles he had placed around the room that made it look like a temple.

He lifted me onto the bed. I could feel my heart racing, my breathing accelerating, and my body yielding.

The morning found us in each other's arms, exhausted but happy, and for the next three days, he stayed home. Even if we wanted to go somewhere for our honeymoon, we couldn't, not in the middle of a bloody revolution. However, I could not imagine being anywhere else. He made me forget about the world.

Every morning, I was served breakfast in bed: a cup of *café con leche* and a piece of buttery toasted bread and slices of chorizo. He watched me eat it with a smile on his face.

"My beautiful girl from Arroyo Blanco," he said with pride.

I wish he could have stayed home longer, but there was too much work at the port.

When on day four, he dressed for work, had breakfast, and kissed me before he left home, I realized that my life as a housewife had started.

Chapter 14 – A New Life

A couple of hours later, I was looking around the kitchen trying to figure out what to cook when I heard someone at the door. "Anybody there? Madeline, this is Rita." Listening to these words made me smile as I rushed towards the door. When I opened it, I gave the middle-aged woman a warm embrace. We kissed each other on the cheek as she held on to a plate of fritters.

"Here, this is my honeymoon gift for the two of you. Not that I like to show off, but I make the best fritters in town."

I took the plate and placed it on the dining room table.

Tía Rita, Willy's aunt, had met me during my introduction to the town, but we didn't have much time to talk then.

We sat down in the two rocking chairs that furnished my tiny living room. I offered her coffee, but she said she had already drunk two cups that day.

She asked me many questions about my parents, my sister, and the life I left behind. Her receptiveness impressed me.

"You love your father more than your mother, don't you?" she asked.

I nodded. She wanted to know why, but I wasn't ready to tell her.

For the next few days, she invited Willy and me for dinner and taught me how to cook. She said she felt alone because her husband was traveling.

I spent most of my time at her house talking to her about what was happening with the rebels and learning about each other's families.

One morning, when I arrived at her house, she opened the door and kissed me, but something didn't look right. As we sat in her living room, she seemed lost in thought.

"Is everything okay?" I asked.

She responded with a faint, unconvincing yes.

I then heard a noise in the back of the house. Moments later, a tall, big man wearing an undershirt and a pair of shorts approached us with a big smile.

"Hey, look who's here! You must be Madi. Oye chica, my wife said you were pretty, but you're so much more. You're on fire. Come on. Give your new uncle a hug."

I looked at his wife with a timid expression, rose from my chair, and extended my hand to shake his. However, he pulled me towards him, gave me a tight hug, and grabbed my rear with his hands. When I felt the firm squeeze, I quickly stepped back.

"Madi, this is Antonio, my husband," Tía Rita said in a monotone voice.

"Rita, can you go to the kitchen and bring me a cup of café con leche?" Antonio said staring at me.

I looked at Rita in panic. She hesitated for a moment.

"I'll be right back," she said.

When his wife was gone, his eyes focused on my bosom.

"You are more beautiful than any woman I've ever seen. It's hard to get my eyes off you."

I crossed my arms and gave him an angry look.

"You should be ashamed of yourself," I whispered. "How could you speak to me that way with your wife just a few meters away? Besides, I'm a married woman."

"Ah! That doesn't mean much. Married, single. It makes no difference. How old are you?"

"Eighteen."

"Nice."

I could hear the increasing sound of footsteps, but it didn't seem to matter to him. He kept undressing me with his eyes. When she returned with the cup of café con leche and gave it to her husband, I grabbed my purse.

"Tía Rita," I said, "I have a lot to do today. I should go home."

I kissed her on the cheek and left without looking at him.

After that encounter, I only returned to Rita's house when I knew her husband was away. The way he treated her saddened me. As mad as I was at Antonio, telling Willy was not an option. I didn't want an altercation between my husband and Antonio.

Antonio was away frequently, as he conducted a train between different parts of the province and the port, a job that afforded him and Rita with a very comfortable lifestyle. Their only son was mute. As much as she enjoyed talking, I could only imagine how painful it was to have a son who could never tell her how much he loved her.

Thanks to Rita's teachings, within only a few days, I began to prepare the most delicious meals. She also showed me how to make guava marmalade and her tasty cod fritters.

We didn't speak about the incident at her house until one sunny afternoon, when I was sitting in a hammock on her front porch, and she told me about her unfaithful husband.

She said she had decided to look the other way because she was already too old to start over.

I wondered if, when I turned her age, I would have to worry about infidelity. I could never tolerate it but refrained from passing judgement. Our conversation then changed to my mother. She wanted to understand why we didn't get along.

I told her about the smacks on the head I had endured and my fear of her when I was growing up.

"Sometimes, parents are difficult to understand," she said. "You're right to want to leave that in the past. You're a married woman now. One day, you will have your own children, and I'm sure those experiences will help you understand how not to act with your children."

She always had something wise to say, but for me having children seemed far away. I was afraid to bring a child into the world while the revolution was in progress.

Chapter 15 – The Death Camps

Narrator: Madeline

The rebels now controlled the section between Guayabal and Arroyo Blanco, so I could no longer visit my parents as access between the two towns became restricted.

The situation kept deteriorating day by day, with frequent confrontations between the government forces and the rebels, and the rebel-takeover of multiple key sections of Camagüey.

One afternoon, when I was finishing Willy's dinner, I heard a girl screaming my name. I lifted my head and looked through the window. I saw eight-year-old Sarita, the daughter of one of our neighbors, standing by the fence. The thin girl with shoulder-length blond hair waved at me with a fearful look on her face.

"Hurry up, Madeline! Get out! A plane is coming to bomb this area. Hurry!"

"How do you know?" I asked.

"A messenger told my mom. Hurry!"

I quickly dried my hands and rushed out, leaving the door open.

Chapter 15 – The Death Camps

We had been running for a couple of minutes when I heard a loud engine noise, but I couldn't see anything at first because my view was obstructed by trees. As the noise intensified, I kept searching for its source. Once we cleared an area of tall trees, I saw a black airplane appear. It was flying low, coming right towards us. The deafening sound of machine guns then followed. Were they shooting at us? I never felt death as close as I did that day. I could hear people screaming, but I didn't know where the screams were coming from. Then I realized they were coming from the ground.

I hardly had enough time to jump into the hole. Everything happened so fast. I remembered the plane flying above my head and someone pulling me and the girl down, as machine gun fire kept falling at an undeterminable distance that to me felt like only a few meters away. People around me were screaming that the rebels were going to bomb the port. Many thoughts rushed through my head. I worried about Willy, my parents, my little sister, Aunt Rosita, Aunt Rita, and my grandparents. Before everything went black, I imagined them shot dead on a field of white *campanilla* flowers, their clothes stained by their blood.

I didn't know how long I remained unconscious. When I opened my eyes, Willy was bending over the hole, his hands trying to reach my face. People all around me were leaving the bomb shelter, one by one, except Sarita's parents, Lilia and Jorge, who were looking at me with big smiles on their faces.

Chapter 15 – The Death Camps

"Welcome back," Lilia said.

I could no longer hear the airplanes.

"Madeline, look up! It's me. I'm fine. Take my hand."

The moment I saw Willy's smile, I started to cry. He pulled me out of the hole and embraced me.

"It's over, my love. It's over," he said, kissing my tearful face.

I realized later that Sarita had led me to the shelter Willy had helped her father build. I didn't know then that Jorge was one of the rebels and had sent a message to his wife alerting her of the attack. Regardless of how we felt about the rebels, we had to be careful. Most people in the country supported them.

A few months later, on December 31, 1958, Sarita's parents invited Willy and me to welcome the New Year at their house. I thought about my parents so much that evening, especially when the clock hit midnight and all the adults lifted their wine glasses. Later, while Willy and I hugged and kissed each other on the cheek, I prayed for the end of the war. I didn't understand much about politics, but I was tired of seeing men who had been born in the same country kill each other like animals on the streets of my town.

That night, while we slept, President Fulgencio Batista fled the country. On January 1, 1959, Cuba awoke to face a new reality. Bearded men dressed in olive-green uniforms came from the mountains and joined the celebration. The rebels had won, and the people organized parties to celebrate their victory.

A few days later, Antonio, one of Willy's cousins who sympathized with the rebels, came to our house.

"Consider yourselves arrested," Antonio said with a serious expression.

At first, we thought that someone had caught Willy talking bad about the government. After all, people in his family knew that he didn't agree with the rebels.

We looked at Antonio, saddened that he had decided to turn us in. With resignation, we followed him as instructed, while we held hands and waited for the worst.

Moments later, Antonio stopped in front of Rita's house, which was full of neighbors who were celebrating the victory. Antonio turned to us and smiled.

"I had you there for a moment, didn't I?" he asked. He then embraced Willy. "Come on brother; today, all is forgotten. Today, we are all the same."

His words had a strange impact on me, and I didn't know why.

We joined the celebration but exchanged glances with each other throughout the festivities. I didn't trust Antonio or the rebels. Later, I understood why, when the rebels began to visit the houses of those who had opposed them and took the men in buses to death camps. They would all be shot.

Chapter 15 – The Death Camps

Many of the rebel sympathizers gathered in the camps to witness the shootings, including many women with their infant children in their arms.

Overnight, the island became a killing camp.

I was afraid for my father. It wasn't until a month later that Willy and I were able to travel to Arroyo Blanco to visit him. By then, many of Batista's sympathizers had been taken from their houses or fled. The rebels appropriated their houses and belongings.

Every day, Willy grew more vocal of his disagreement with the new government, leading to fights between some members of his family and him. I worried that if he continued to speak his mind, he would end up at a death camp.

Chapter 16 – The Revolution

Narrator: Madeline

A massive exodus—with approximately 1.4 million people leaving the island to immigrate to the Unites States—and public shootings of those who opposed the revolution characterized the first few years of the new administration. By the end of 1960, the government had nationalized most businesses.

During this period, I began to pay more attention to politics and what was happening in the country. Until then, living with my parents had blinded me to what was going on around me. The blindfold had been removed.

The reality of the new government never became more palpable than on the last Sunday of October 1960 when Willy and I went to visit my father. Three weeks earlier, on August 6, the Macareño Industrial Corporation of New York had been nationalized, along with the telephone and electric companies, and 36 sugar mills owned by the United States. My father refused to work for the government.

Chapter 16 – The Revolution

On the day the American owners were scheduled to return to the United States, my father's bosses stopped by. "As you know, we lost the company and everything we had," Mr. Dutch said. "It was a pleasure to have worked with someone like you. We hope to return soon. We'll miss you." Handshakes, tears, and hugs ensued.

My father didn't want to stay at the house the revolutionaries stole from the company that gave him so much, so he left and went to live with his father in his farm. A few weeks later, my grandparents' lands, tools, and cattle were nationalized. At first, the revolutionaries allowed my grandfather to keep a cow. Later, it was confiscated.

Everyone tried to hide what was going on from my grandmother, but she soon figured it out. She no longer had workers who could bring her cigarettes, so every time someone came to visit, she would ask "can you give me a cigarette?" Dementia was taking over her mind. Her husband's health also began to deteriorate. He became so sick and depressed, he no longer had the strength to get off his chair.

One day, he looked at me, grabbed my hand, and said, "My dear granddaughter, I know what these people are doing to us is hard to see. You must be strong."

Unable to endure what was happening to the farm where he had worked so hard, watching the mismanagement by the new government, and enduring the ridicule by some of the townspeople—who laughed at him because his land was taken away—took a toll on my grandfather. He looked so frail; we all thought he would go first. Yet, Grandma always told everyone she didn't want to die before him.

Despite my grandmother's dementia, she somehow sensed her husband's days were numbered. One night, she withered away in her sleep. Grandpa couldn't continue to live in the house he had shared with the love of his life, so he moved to Tia Rosita's house. Twelve days after his beloved wife took her last breath, he joined her in heaven.

My grandfather's body was taken to the farmhouse where he and Grandma had lived, and the family came to pay their final respects. As he lay inside a casket in the living room, Sultán, his loyal dog, howled throughout the night, a sound that could make the skin of the devil himself crawl.

Chapter 17 – The Labor Camps

Narrator: Willy

After the new government established a system called "*azucar a granel*" and eliminated the use of jute sacs for transporting sugar, I lost my job. The sugar began to be loaded through a system of tubes that made the process more efficient.

When I was fired, my brother Julio, who worked in La Ciudad de Camagüey at the Departamento of Repoblación Forestal—a government department dedicated to planting trees throughout the province—got me a job there. So, Madeline and I moved from the Port of Guayabal to the city.

The Ciudad de Camagüey, the crown-jewel of the province that bore the same name, was very different from any other place I knew. People around the country called it *La Ciudad de los Tinajones*.

Tinajones are big, clay-color jars with large openings designed for catching the rain. Produced in massive quantities in the seventeenth century, they became the symbol of Camagüey. Almost every home in the city had at least one.

Chapter 17 – The Labor Camps

The city had several colonial-era, well-kept buildings that made it look majestic, so different from the small-town feel of Arroyo Blanco.

By the time we moved, my brother Julio still believed in the new government, but soon that would change.

As the revolution strengthened its control of the country, Cuba became more dependent on the Soviet Union, and in 1961, Castro declared in front of the world that he was a Marxist-Leninist. At that moment, my brothers realized they had to leave Cuba.

In April 1961, over 1,300 Cuban exiles trained by the CIA landed near the Bay of Pigs with the goal of overthrowing Fidel Castro's government. A few of them were killed, the others captured. Then, the raids began.

I always minded my own business, that is, if no one messed with my family, so I didn't understand why I was one of the thousands of men who were arrested that day. My poor, sweet Madeline screamed, cried, and held on to me, so the soldiers wouldn't take me.

A group of forty-seven men, myself included, were taken to a prison at the Central Francisco and placed inside a room that measured about ten square feet. The place was so small we had to sleep standing up. We kept our shoes on as our feet became swollen. If we had taken them off, we wouldn't have been able to put them back on.

During the first two days, we had casual conversations with each other. When by the

Chapter 17 – The Labor Camps

third day we had not been fed any food, we came to the realization we needed to conserve our energy, so we stopped talking.

The hunger caused so much pain in our stomachs that it made us buckle. We drank as much water as we could, hoping that would make us feel full. After a while, numbness set in.

On day six, a lieutenant arrived to survey the conditions at Central Francisco. The black man with kind eyes must have realized that unless our living conditions improved, we would begin to die off. He asked if any of the imprisoned men had a farm, and if so, if they would be willing to bring food to us. One of the imprisoned men whose family lived near the camp agreed to provide it, and for the next five days, we were fed milk and bread every day.

On the same day the lieutenant arrived, Madeline and my mother came to visit me. They both burst into tears when they saw me.

"Many men are imprisoned all over the province," Madeline said. "So many have been jailed that parks have been turned into prisons and surrounded by live wires."

She said all but three of my brothers had been jailed.

"Why did you come?" I asked. I didn't want them to see me in my condition.

"No one can stop me from seeing you, my son," my mother said. "I'm going to visit all of your jailed brothers."

"Go home, Mamá."

They stood there, watching me from afar until a guard ordered them to leave.

During one of the nights we spent in the small cell, an airplane passed by. The men guarding us must have thought it was an unfriendly airplane. Immediately, two machine guns were placed, one on each side of our room, between the metal bars. None of us thought we would survive the night. One of the men in our group was so frightened, he collapsed.

We were released eleven days following our arrival.

During my sixteen-kilometer trip home, I counted my blessings. If that lieutenant had not arrived in time, we would have died of starvation. I later heard that when militia leaders heard what he had done, he was accused of being a traitor and shot to death.

On my way home, I walked through unpaved country roads and forests. Exhausted, I stopped at a small house I found along the way to ask for water.

I had become unrecognizable from the little food and sleepless nights, but all I was thinking about when I left my captors was Madeline. The thought of her hazel eyes and beautiful smile and the urge to have her in my arms again kept me alive and motivated my swollen legs to keep moving.

The more I walked, the more my legs and feet hurt. My shoes were still on, but they hardly fit from the swelling, making each step increasingly unbearable. I took small breaks along the way, sitting on big rocks or under trees.

After a while, the sun began to set on the horizon. I don't know how many hours I walked. Judging by the position of the sun when I left, more than five.

As I approached our house, a spurt of energy came over me, and I began to walk faster. "Madeline," I kept telling myself.

She didn't know I was coming home. Given the way I looked, I didn't want to scare her. I needed to hurry, hoping to get home before she went to bed.

The front door was locked when I arrived, and I didn't have my keys. I looked through the windows and saw her in a rocking chair, a lit candle on a small table next to her. She had fallen asleep. I went around the house and found an open window. I climbed in. Looking and smelling like death, I walked towards Madeline and stood in front of her, afraid to touch her.

"Madeline," I whispered.

She moved slightly in her chair. I called her name again. When she opened her eyes, a look of terror transformed her expression. She was about to scream, when I said, "It's me, Willy."

As dirty as I was, she jolted out of her seat and embraced me. At first, she cried in my arms.

"I'm fine, Madeline. It's over."

She wept some more, and when she was able to speak, the first words out of her mouth

105

were, "Thank you God, for bringing him back to me!"

We walked to our bedroom, and she helped me remove my shoes. The moment they came off, I could feel the fluid traveling from my legs to my feet, and as I looked around me, I couldn't believe I was home.

While I showered, Madeline prepared me a warm meal. It felt good to feel the water running over my body after so many days without a proper shower. As the memories of the past several days rushed through my mind, I wept out of anger. I closed my fists and slammed the walls. I didn't fulfill the promise I made to Madeline's father, and I didn't think I would be able to keep her safe if we stayed in Cuba.

Madeline and I spoke for a long time that night, until we fell asleep in each other's arms.

When I woke up the next morning, she told me about my brother Leo. She and my mother went to visit him after his release from the work camp. Not only was he as thin as I had become, but he had stopped being the man she once knew. He approached her very slowly.

"Do you know anything about Willy?" he asked.

She told him she had visited me.

"He's dead! I know he's dead! They killed him. Those sons of bitches killed him."

She feared he had lost his mind. All Madeline could do was cry when she told me about it. We later learned he had endured psychological torture. His captors described in detail how each of his brothers had died. They

106

also put an empty gun to his head several times and pulled the trigger. He had endured other horrible experiences he would never share with anyone. However, he did say that the physical and psychological torture continued for several days until he became afraid of his own shadow.

Chapter 18 – My Friend, Marino

Narrator: Willy

After my release from jail, I began to work at Marino Garcia's farm. He owned a colony and several acres of land and dedicated himself to livestock and sugarcane.

Marino, eighty-five, of Spanish descent, and very generous, was well known for his support of the communist system. Over the years he lived in Cuba, he purchased lands and created a profitable enterprise. One of his proudest accomplishments was to be able to provide meals for the men who worked for him.

When Castro came to power, Marino's workers joined the revolution. At the time, many lived in the colony. One of them, Tony, was known for bringing prostitutes and pimping them to other men. Tony reported Marino to the authorities, falsely claiming he didn't provide food for his workers.

Marino gave food vouchers only to the men who worked. Tony, busy with his prostitution business, refused to do anything else.

The day Marino's apprehension order came in, I waited for him at the entrance of the farm. When I saw the lights of his Jeep approaching, I waved my arms in front of it. I then told him about the arrest order. Inside his colony, the authorities were planning to tie him by his hands and bring him on foot to the police station of Central Francisco, located sixteen kilometers away. I knew Marino was in no condition to make the journey, so I wanted to spare him the embarrassment and aggravation.

After I told him about the arrest order, Marino ordered his driver to take him to the police station, where he turned himself in. He explained his practice of giving food vouchers only to those who worked. However, he offered to provide food to everyone who lived in his colony if the revolution agreed to pay for half of the cost. The police chief was not interested but released him.

Sometime later, Marino's lands were taken by the revolution. He was only able to keep his house and a small parcel of land behind his home.

Half of Marino's children traveled to the United States, a slap on the face to someone who once opposed capitalism. Marino's health could not endure the loss of everything for which he had worked.

I never knew how he died. People said he had an agonizing death, but despite the years that have passed since I met him, I never forgot this man betrayed by the system he so blindly believed in.

Chapter 19 - Guillermito

Narrator: Madeline

Willy and I had just finished our dinner when we heard someone knock. I started to pick up the dishes, while Willy went to the living room to check who it was. Moments later, I heard the familiar voice and rejoined Willy.

"What a surprise!" I said, giving my brother-in-law Enrique a hug. He was standing in front of Willy, holding a large black bag. He wore a black t-shirt matching the color of shorts. "Let me bring you some coffee," I added.

"I'm in a hurry. There's a boat waiting near the Port of Guayabal to take me out of Cuba. There's some space for the two of you. Why don't you come with me?"

His concern for Willy touched me, but I couldn't leave without saying goodbye to the most important people in my life. His sudden decision to flee didn't surprise me. Enrique had been organizing a group of men to join him at the Sierra de Cubitas, one of the few mountainous areas in Camagüey. He planned to organize a resistance against the Castro government, joining another group that already waited, hidden in caves, in these mountains. Enrique explained that someone from the G2, Cuba's secret forces, infiltrated Enrique's group and reported him to the authorities. However, a revolutionary woman who liked him sent him a message. An order had been issued for his arrest. If he didn't leave right away, he would risk facing the firing squad.

Willy looked at me with hesitation, and I shook my head. With disappointment in his eyes, Willy turned to his brother and said, "No, if it were me alone, I would go, but I can't put Madi in danger. Don't worry about us."

Enrique embraced his brother, then me.

"We'll see each other again soon," he said. "Be careful, and don't tell anyone I came here tonight."

After Enrique left, we sat in the living room for a while. We feared his presence at our house had placed us in danger. What if someone was following him?

By then, Mauricio, another brother, had abandoned Cuba on a boat and resided in Jamaica. Mauricio left with Captain Ubaldo Reina, who, although part of the new revolutionary government, decided to leave with his family after Castro declared his allegiance to communism. On the night Captain Reina left, still wearing his military uniform, he ordered the men guarding the port to go back to their homes because they needed to rest and get ready for an invasion the following day. The men believed him and abandoned their posts. The story of the captain who turned into a deserter and left with Mauricio would be repeated by Willy and his brothers for years to come.

Enrique would join Mauricio in Jamaica. Both had left their wives in Cuba with plans to get them out as soon as they could. Cirilo, the first brother to leave, had flown out of Cuba with his wife and son. His wife, a judge with close connections to the Batista government, facilitated the trip through her connections and under the auspices of the United States government.

A couple of months after Enrique left, we presented our papers to leave Cuba. By then, we had lost hope I would get pregnant, as we had been trying for three years.

Three months after we applied for our passports, I started to get sick in the mornings. This continued for a few days, so I visited the doctor. He informed us that our dream to become parents would soon become a reality. As much as I wanted to be a mother, I worried my pregnancy would delay our trip.

I had never seen my mother as happy as when she heard the news. After that day, she began to treat me as a daughter.

Around this time, my sister Nancy moved in with me to attend school in the city. She had already turned twelve but had not lost the cheerfulness and kindness of the child who asked me to defend myself when I lived with my parents. Her move and the upcoming birth provided excuses for my parents to visit me more frequently.

As my due date neared, my mother reminded us we needed baby furniture. My father offered to help, but Willy wanted to prove himself to him. "Thank you, Victorino. I'll handle it," he said.

A week later, after going to every store and talking to the neighbors, he came home with a look of disappointment. There were no cribs at the stores.

"I'll talk to my father," I said.

Dad had amassed a good amount of money during the time he worked for the Americans. Money opened doors. Still, Willy refused my father's help.

During a family gathering, we learned that one of Willy's cousins had plans to leave Cuba. When he heard we needed baby furniture, he donated a crib and a dresser to us. The day Willy brought them home, he kissed me and gave me a big hug.

"See? I told your father I would take care of everything."

"Yes, you did!"

On July 20, 1961, our son, Guillermito, was born at the Colonia Española de Camagüey. The moment the nurse placed him in my arms was the happiest of my life. Our parents came to visit him. Until then, the two sets of parents had not connected as a family. My father still thought I deserved someone better. Our son became the bridge that would join them.

Chapter 19 - Guillermito

That beautiful baby, who at first appeared so full of life, soon became very ill. I could not satisfy his hunger with my own milk and had to give him any milk I could find. Unable to tolerate it, he began having frequent diarrhea and spent most of the time going from hospital to hospital. I felt inadequate as a mother, unable to sustain the life of my own son. During the long hours I stayed by his side praying for a miracle, he looked at me, as if asking me for help. All I could do was tell him "I'm sorry."

One of his doctors gave me some hope when he suggested a medication that could save him. When I heard it wasn't available in Cuba, I called Enrique and asked him to send it from Jamaica. Meanwhile, I prayed that my son could stay alive long enough.

One night, the nurse came into my son's room at my request because the baby wouldn't stop crying. I yelled at her, "Please do something!"

The nurse looked at me and patted me on the back. "Sweetheart," she said. "You need to let him go. It's time."

"How dare you!"

The nurse shook her head and looked down while I caressed Guillermito and prayed. After a while, his crying stopped. As if something had occurred to her, the nurse took a couple of steps towards my son and waved her hand in front of his eyes. He didn't blink. His eye stayed wide open, full of tears, his discomfort discoloring his face. I held his hands in mine. "Why isn't he blinking?" I asked, trying to hold back the tears.

"He's lost his vision."

I looked at her in shock, mouth agape, then bent over my son's little body and wept.

By the time the medication arrived, our son's body laid at a funeral home.

If his birth was the brightest day of my life, losing him was the darkest. I had not left his side for days. I wanted him to feel the love of his parents while he could. I didn't want him to fear or to feel alone.

When our son took his last breath, I held him in my arms for a long time, while Willy sat on a chair by my side, weeping.

At first, I couldn't accept he was gone, not even after his spirit left his body, and he became a shell of what he was. I wanted to join him so he wouldn't be lonely. I wanted to assure him I would always be by his side, protecting him. Then I began to acknowledge his passing. Losing my child felt as if my skin and my insides had been ripped apart.

My son remained in my arms almost thirty minutes. The nurse then returned, touched my shoulder, and asked me to give him to her.

"I'm calling the funeral home," she said. "Let me take him from you, and they will take him there. Do you have family in the area? You should ask them to accompany you."

Willy rose from his chair, wiped his tears, and stared at the nurse in a threatening manner.

"That's my son!" he yelled. "Who the hell are you to tell me what's best for *my* son? He's not going anywhere."

He took the baby from me and rocked him in his arms.

"Don't worry. I won't leave you alone. Don't be afraid."

The nurse and I looked at each other. Seeing Willy in that state led me to conclude I had lost them both.

I heard someone say that people don't know how strong they are unless being strong is their only choice. I had to reach deep down and pull strength from inside me. My son needed me one last time.

It was almost midnight when I left La Colonia Española on foot. No one roamed the streets at the time, and my tears clouded my vision. The chalet homes in this nice area of town had the porch lights off. I had always admired their manicured gardens, but on this night, nothing gave me joy. For a moment, I didn't know what to do, or where to go. Then I realized that Mauricio's wife didn't live far. I needed to talk to her, to someone. If she could come with me, Willy might listen to her. My legs felt heavy as I walked the three blocks. When I arrived, I noticed all the lights were off. I knocked on the door several times. No one answered.

Many thoughts ran through my mind as I walked back to the hospital. I had so many dreams for my baby boy. He would never feel the joy of taking his first steps, of eating solid foods, of playing in the sun, of kissing a girl, or having children. He came to this world for three months to show me how it felt to love him and how hard it was to let him go.

After not finding anyone at Mauricio's house, I walked back to the hospital. By the time I arrived, I noticed a van from the funeral home in front of the building. Willy stood by the passenger door and the nurse by his side.

"What's going on?" I asked.

"Your husband insisted in accompanying your son to the funeral home," she said. "The two of you can go in the front, and your son will be in the back. They will take good care of him."

***

Willy wasn't the same after our son died. This forced me to become stronger than I ever thought I could be. Before that night, I thought I needed a man to protect me and give me value, but losing a child showed me my inner strength and resiliency. Willy would never be able to talk about our son again without falling apart. He would always remember the sadness in our son's eyes, his desperate pleas for help, and our inability to do anything to save him.

Chapter 20 – Hurricane Flora

Narrator: Madeline

The news spread all over our town like dust on a windy day. After moving over the island of Grenada, Hurricane Flora slammed into Haiti as a Category 4. Cuba was next, and our province stood right on its path. In Haiti, high winds and a twelve-foot storm surge destroyed coastal towns, and news reports estimated a death toll of over 3,000 people.

Willy and I listened to the frequent radio announcements. Winds were expected to pick up once the storm crossed the stretch of ocean between Haiti and southeastern Cuba. We feared for our families.

On October 4, 1963, Flora made landfall 48 kilometers east of Guantánamo Bay as a Category 3 hurricane.

Pompeyo, one of our neighbors, went house by house asking people to come to his house to weather the storm.

"Are you planning to stay here?" he would ask each neighbor. "Are you crazy? Come over to our house. We can help each other if we stay together."

Chapter 20 – Hurricane Flora

Almost everyone who lived on our block, including many of our friends, left their homes and gathered at Pompeyo's house, one of the largest ones in the area. He lived there with his wife, Mercedes. The wooden home had a thatched roof and polished cement floors.

Pompeyo held a high-level position with the new administration, but he built his house before Castro came to power. Prior to leaving our home, Willy grabbed one of chickens and put it in a bag. He gave it to Mercedes as a gift. Other people brought rice.

As families began to arrive, they sat on wooden chairs arranged all over the ample living and dining rooms. Mercedes loved to talk and lift people's spirits. Despite having opposed political views, I found her sense of humanity refreshing. During the last few days of my son's life, she and her husband had come to the hospital to join me in prayer, a gesture I never forgot. Castro's government didn't support the practice of religion, which made their prayers more meaningful.

Mercedes's generosity came through on this day as well. She went to the kitchen and made coffee for everyone, making us feel like relatives.

An hour after our arrival, noticing that winds were picking up, Pompeyo asked for volunteers to help him secure the roof. Willy and some of the other men offered to help. When they finished, they came back soaked from the heavy downpour.

Chapter 20 – Hurricane Flora

It rained for hours, sometimes heavier than others. That evening, we heard the radio announcement: "Rivers are overflowing." As soon as it concluded, we lost electricity.

That day, Mercedes had prepared a large feast of yellow rice and chicken that she cooked on her gas stove.

By the second day, the food had run out. At first, people distracted themselves by playing dominoes and telling each other stories, but as the hours passed, they became restless.

People's nervousness grew after Pompeyo came into the living room wearing a raincoat and announced he was on his way to the airport tower to get an update on the situation. We thought he had lost his mind. The winds were blowing with force now, bending small trees in front of the house and making it unsafe to be outside. Mercedes begged him not to go, but the stocky fifty-something-year-old wouldn't listen.

After Pompeyo left, some of us kept looking through the windows, hoping for his safe return. About an hour later, the door opened, and Pompeyo came in.

"I have the latest news!" he announced. "The storm is stationary now, and it's anyone's guess what's going to happen next. We are on our own."

His sense of responsibility for his fellow men poured out of him.

"Don't worry. We'll get through this."

Chapter 20 – Hurricane Flora

The storm remained over the island for a long time, causing a levee to break in the northern portion of the province.

Once hurricane-force winds reached us, and the roof began shake, all the women and children started to scream. We later would learn that guava-sized hail had killed people in other parts of the province. As I heard the roaring winds, I started to pray. Some of the women joined me.

"God doesn't exist. Don't waste your time," one of the men said and laughed at us.

"You shouldn't laugh," Willy said.

The man waved his hand in dismissal. Moments later, big balls of hail began to slam the roof. It may have been a coincidence, but the man fell to his knees and asked God for forgiveness.

Within our group was the son of a Mexican woman who kept a list of the birthdays of everyone in the neighborhood. He organized impromptu neighborhood parties to celebrate them. It didn't matter to him if people wanted their birthdays acknowledged or not, or if they had suffered a loss around that time and didn't want a celebration. He threw them a party anyways, with him as the entertainment. He sang and played his guitar, while people gathered around him and danced. Some would hide from him or stayed at the movie theater until past midnight to avoid him. However, during the storm, his singing and playing helped relieve some of the stress.

Chapter 20 – Hurricane Flora

I can't recall how long we remained at Pompeyo's house. Perhaps three days. During that time, I wondered about my family and Willy's. I couldn't wait until the communication was restored. When, at last, Hurricane Flora cleared the province, and it became safe to go out again, a group of men surveyed the surroundings, looking for fallen cows in nearby farms. Local authorities had allowed people to cook any cow that had fallen during the storm. That allowed our group to have a great feast of beef and *mofongo* that satiated our hunger.

On the day we returned to our homes, we thanked Pompeyo for his hospitality. Sometime later, the divisions among those who wanted to leave and those who supported Castro returned.

Hurricane Flora became one of the worst weather systems to hit Cuba, deepening the economic crises that affected the island.

Chapter 21- I Want my Dad

Narrator: Madeline

Every day after work, Willy sat on the edge of our bed and looked at the empty crib for an hour. Meanwhile, I read the most recent Bohemia magazine, sitting on an upholstered bamboo rocking chair that was part of a living room set my grandfather gave me as a wedding present. It had two comfortable seats called *butacas*, two rocking chairs, and a square coffee table with a glass top.

Each night, the moment I heard the shower running, I would go to the kitchen to warm up our dinner. Then, we sat down to eat and talk about what I had read or heard on the radio. I also shared with Willy any relevant news about our family. We didn't talk about our son. Each one of us kept him in our hearts and suffered his loss in silence, except for those moments in which parents passed by with a baby in a stroller, or we heard an infant cry. Those were the hardest moments. "I miss him," I would say and take refuge in my husband's arms.

***

It was 1964, at the beginning of November. Fidel Castro had just announced that Cuba would have a socialist constitution by 1969 or sooner, and Willy felt uneasy. He wanted to abandon Cuba as soon possible, even if we had to leave by boat. Before his plans could take shape, an unexpected news took us by surprise.

Over two years had passed since we'd lost the baby, and by this time I thought I would not get pregnant again. God knows how much we had tried. When my period didn't come for a couple of months, I thought that my stress was to blame, but before long, I noticed physical changes. A visit to the Colonia Española Clinic confirmed my suspicion. I was pregnant.

As much as we wanted to leave Cuba, we both realized that this plan would have to be placed on hold. The news also meant that we would have to use a legal way to travel abroad.

When Willy came from work and I told him I was two months pregnant, he alternated between periods of laughter and tears. Months later, as my pregnancy progressed, he became more and more fearful that the baby would not survive, which made him obsessive about my health. His family helped procure the food he bought for me in the black market. He wanted to make sure I had the appropriate nutrition, no matter what the economic conditions were.

At the end of April 1965, when my contractions began, Mercedes, Pompeyo's wife, stopped by the house. I suspected that her visit wasn't that of a friend, but of someone hoping to learn any details that could compromise members of our family. I didn't realize at the time that the slight pain I was feeling in my lower back had anything to do with my pregnancy.

Nancy was in class at that time. I couldn't believe how much she had changed since she moved in with us. A couple weeks before, I had organized a small party for her Sweet Fifteen celebration at my house, and she seemed so grown-up and assertive. She had an exotic beauty with long black hair and a lighter complexion than I. At the time of her party, I didn't know that she had been dating a neighborhood boy in secret. To spend more time with her, he enrolled in the typing classes Nancy was taking.

On the day the contractions started, I couldn't wait for Nancy to return from school, but everything happened so fast. As my pain worsened, Mercedes concluded that the baby was coming soon and ran out of our house to find someone who could take me to the hospital by car. Later, after leaving my house in a neighbor's car, we stopped by Willy's new job, a local cement factory. By then, Willy had been fired from his job at the Department of Reforestation after the government learned that everyone in his family was leaving Cuba.

The baby would not wait for our families. Thirty minutes after my arrival, Phil Enrique was born. His first name came from one of

Willy's friends. He didn't want to name our second son the same as our first. Willy's friend, Phil, was a successful young man with a college education who opposed Castro as much as Willy did. The second, from one of Willy's brothers, the one who went out of his way to send the medicine for Guillermito, even if the medicine had arrived too late.

Phil was the most beautiful boy I had ever seen with chubby cheeks and a beaming smile. He didn't have much hair on his head, but his eyes were darker and bigger than his father's and possessed an intensity that conveyed intelligence. My mother laughed at me when I said he looked smart. She said it was my motherly blindness that made me see him that way. I knew time would prove me right.

After the first couple of weeks, Phil began to sleep through the night. His father would get out of bed every couple of hours, stand by his crib, and place his finger under his nose to make sure he was breathing. Then he returned to bed. Afraid Phil was going to die, he did this until the baby was six months old, but our second son was strong and healthy. By his sixth month of life, he could say *mamá* and *papá*.

As I explored all that was happening around us, I wondered what kind of life my son would live in Cuba.

In November of 1965, the opening of UMAP (Military Units to Aid Production)— forced labor camps to which the adult children of the upper middle class, homosexuals, conscientious objectors of the revolution, intellectuals, and Christians were taken—broadcasted that Cuba had taken a destructive path.

Over 30,000 men were taken to these camps and forced to work ten to twelve hours a day. They ate rice and spoiled food, drank contaminated water, and lived in overcrowded barracks with no electricity, latrines, or showers. Many men committed suicide, including the son of a friend of my father's. I feared for my son's future.

At twenty months, Phil spoke in short sentences. Every time I entered his room, his smile gave me life, making me forget at times how much we had lost under the new government. We could no longer speak openly against Castro and the revolution. The government controlled the media and scarcity became an everyday reality. An increasing paranoia had led to countless killings. And yet, somehow, in the middle of all this, our son gave us a reason to feel happy, but this tarnished happiness was not meant to last.

On the day our lives unraveled, Willy arrived from work earlier than usual with a letter in his hand. Our two-year-old was playing in the living room with his favorite red truck, one I purchased after spending an entire night in line. Toys only came to the store once a year. The selection and quantities were limited, so parents had to arrive at the store the night before to secure a spot in line. That red truck was not the best toy that came to the stores that year. It was the best one I could buy when my turn arrived.

The way he looked at me told me something was wrong. He handed me the letter, and I read it in silence. Willy was to report to a specific location that very same day. He was asked to bring with him some work clothes.

"Why do you have to go?" I asked.

"That's the rule. I have no choice."

I knew he was right, but part of me expected a different answer. I told him I would accompany him and, while he showered, I rushed to the kitchen to serve him his dinner. Later, we took the bus to the address on the letter.

When the bus left us near our destination, and I noticed the vast military presence on the street and the numerous families all around, I knew something was wrong. It felt as if the entire province was there. The men stood in line as instructed by police, their families next to them. I stood by Willy with my son in my arms. The rumor of what was about to happen spread through the line quickly. When I saw the lady in front of me hugging her husband and crying, I asked her what was going on.

"They are taking them away," she said.

"Where?"

"I don't know," she replied. "They're taking them all away."

My hands turned clammy. Willy embraced the baby and me and assured me that everything would be okay, but the military presence around me suggested otherwise. There were police dogs everywhere and an eerie feeling in the air. The sun was starting to set on the horizon when we got to the front of the line and Willy was ordered to get into one of the trucks. He and I embraced, but two military men ripped Willy from my arms. I screamed "don't take him!" and my two-year-old extended his arms to his father: "My daddy! Don't take my daddy!"

Our son was inconsolable with heavy tears bathing his face while he kept screaming: "I want my dad! I want my dad!"

Chapter 22 – The Labor Camp

Narrator: Madeline

Overnight, many men who, like my husband wanted to leave Cuba, had disappeared with no explanation. I exchanged my contact information with other women whose husbands were taken, but like me, the women ignored their husbands' whereabouts. I prayed every day for his safe return, and not a day went by when my son didn't ask about his father. He displayed a maturity beyond his young years.

He began to draw stick figures representing what had occurred: a boy and a mom holding hands, a dad being taken away. In another drawing, he was beating a policeman with a stick.

After a few days, the need to make money to provide for my son became my biggest imperative, setting aside, to some extent, how I felt about being a single mother with no financial support from her husband. At a time when men worked and women raised the children, I wasn't prepared to sustain a family on my own.

However, people in Cuba said that necessity was the mother of invention. I started to talk to my neighbors about my skills as a seamstress and offered my services, except that I didn't have a sewing machine. Soon, this too would change. My parents came to visit me every two weeks. It was difficult for them to get to my house, as they lived almost two hours away. When I told my mother about how I planned to support myself, she did something I never forgot. At the time, a limited number of sewing machines had arrived in a local store from Czechoslovakia. The long lines and limited supplies made it difficult for me to buy one, but my mother spoke to one of her cousins who had connections. I suspected she paid him a large sum of money, but she never said so. Two days later, he delivered a brand-new sewing machine to my house.

Through word of mouth, my business expanded at a rapid pace, and before long, I found myself sewing day and night. When my parents visited, it pained my father to see me working so hard. He brought money to help me as much as he could, but I kept telling him to keep his money. He needed it for my mom and himself, as he had already retired.

My life became my sewing and my son. He drew or played all day with the few toys he had, especially his favorite red truck, while I sat by my sewing machine for hours at a time.

Chapter 22 – The Labor Camp

One morning, thirty days after Willy's departure, I heard a knock at the door. The pessimist inside me feared the worst. When I opened, I saw a woman I had never seen before, middle-aged, heavy, with pepper hair. She said she was bringing news from my husband. I invited her in and rushed to the kitchen to prepare her a fresh cup of coffee. After drinking it, she opened her purse and handed me a piece of folded paper. I glanced at her, trying to ascertain whether the news on that letter was good or bad. I couldn't tell based on her expression.

I unfolded the sheet of paper and, the moment I saw the handwriting, a sense of relief overcame me for only a few seconds. Then, my preoccupation returned. My heart was beating fast as I started to read:

Dear Madeline,

Since they took me away, I've been thinking about you day and night. The thought of coming back to you and our son is keeping me alive. I don't want to worry you, but they took us to a camp called Las Carolinas where we slept in bunk beds and ate little food. They gave us one meal a day: a piece of boniato and a handful of beans, so few beans that it became a practice to count how many were on our plates, less than what a small child would eat.

They have moved us to another camp called Guillermón.

Chapter 22 – The Labor Camp

We are forced to work all day. The other night, we were picking potatoes until after the sun went down. Here we are only fed once a day, just like in the other camp. I have considered eating raw potatoes, but the soldiers watch us and check our pockets when we leave the fields.

In a couple of weeks, you will be allowed to visit me, but if you can't come, I will understand.

I want you to know that I love you more than I've loved anyone in my life. I dream of the day I can have you in my arms again. Wait for me and tell my son about me. Tell him his daddy loves him.

Love,

Willy

My eyes were full of tears by the time I finished reading his letter, but what she told me made me feel worse.

"I saw your husband standing by a fence, his eyes focused in the distance. He looked as if he had not slept for days and seemed so sad, I felt compelled to approach him. When he told me about you and your son, I offered to bring you this letter. I wouldn't have been able to forgive myself if I didn't."

After talking to that kind woman whose name I've forgotten, I told myself she must have been an angel sent by God. Knowing that

133

my husband was alive and that I would be able to see him energized me, and I began to make the plans for my visit. I asked my family to help me gather as many cans of condensed milk as they could. I cooked them in the pressure cooker for over 40 minutes each to turn the milk into a thick caramel-color custard. I kept crackers and cookies people brought me and cooked guava marmalade. A couple of days before the trip, I kept all the bread that I was entitled to buy, sliced it, and toasted it in a frying pan.

When the day of my trip arrived, I was restless. It was dark when I left the house with a woman whose husband was at the camp. Her name was Concha. I left my son with Nancy, even though he kept yelling at me, telling me he wanted to see his daddy. Nancy had to grab him and restrain him.

After a two-hour bus trip, we were left on a country road in the middle of nowhere. It was a deserted dirt path, the color of clay. Green pastures surrounded us with isolated queen palm trees far in the distance. After the bus disappeared and we could no longer smell the fuel odor that emanated from it or listen to the loud sound of the engine, we gave each other a look that conveyed "now what?"

Concha had asked the bus driver for directions. All he said was "take that road, and you will find it." As we began to walk with heavy loads hanging from each of our shoulders, we couldn't see anything in the distance, other than blue-orange cloudless dawn skies, green grass, and red dirt.

Concha was the eternal optimist and kept telling me that this experience was a small bump in the road, leading to something great. The pessimist in me feared what I would find. When the sun rose on the horizon, we began to sweat. The longer we walked, the heavier our bags felt. Concha, blond, tall, and thin, contrasted with my fuller figure. However, she kept taking deep breaths and seemed more winded than me throughout the long walk. After a while, we began to see a crowd in the distance. By the time we arrived at the entrance of the camp, there was no doubt in my mind that we were at the right place. The gate was open, and the moment I walked in, Concha's husband, a tall, dark-haired man, came running towards us and embraced his wife. I watched them kiss, feeling a little awkward, but there was something about Concha that didn't look right. Her skin began to lose color, and before long, she collapsed in his arms.

He gave her gentle slaps on her face as he placed her body on the ground and kissed her cheek while repeating, "Concha, mi amor, are you okay? Wake up."

Moments later, she opened her eyes. I took a bottle of water I had brought Willy and gave her a sip. When she asked me what happened, all I could come up with was "dehydration," a plausible explanation, considering how long we had been walking.

Chapter 22 – The Labor Camp

"You scared me," I said and gave her a hug.

I was about to leave them alone to search for Willy when I heard someone calling my name. I turned my head and looked up in the distance, noticing a man waving at me and smiling. The features on his face, his hair, and height told me it had to be Willy, but he looked unrecognizable. He weighed 190 pounds when he left the house, and in thirty days, he had lost over twenty pounds. He ran towards me, while I tried to walk as fast as I could. We embraced, trying to keep our emotions in check. No kisses. Willy and I were more guarded in front of others than Concha and her husband and left more intimate shows of affections for private settings.

Concha and her husband joined us for a while. Then, she and I made plans to meet after visiting hours ended.

The time at the camp went by too quickly and instead of leaving me with a sense of relief, it left me in despair. The thought of leaving my husband there, after all the things he told me about the inhumane conditions at the camp, was unbearable.

Willy also told me that the wives of some of the men at the camp had been taken from their homes to perform mandatory labor. If this terrified me, it also changed me. Until now, I had never been able to stand up for anything, but if anyone thought they were going to take my only son away from me, they had to be ready for the fight of their lives. I knew I was.

Chapter 23 - Nancy

Narrator: Madeline

Some of the women in the neighborhood were taken away to work on the fields, and I feared it would only be a matter of time before my turn arrived.

Pompeyo and his wife oversaw the CDR, the Committee of Defense of the Revolution for our block. These committees, created by the government, consisted of a family in each block assigned to monitor and report suspicious activities. If anyone could help me, I knew Pompeyo and his wife could.

I visited Mercedes on a cloudy afternoon when her husband was at work. She invited me in, offered me coffee, and listened to my story.

"But Madeline, they can't take you away. You have a son," she said.

"That doesn't matter to them."

"That's barbaric. I will talk to Pompeyo. Don't worry. We will handle this."

She seemed honest, and I appreciated her concern, but after I left, I wondered if she acted that way only to make me feel better.

Chapter 23 - Nancy

She visited me a couple of times after that day to provide me status reports. Her husband had written two letters to important people he knew explaining I didn't have anyone to care for my son. He also made telephone calls to people who owed him favors, and at last, I received permission to stay home. I thanked them, even offered a free alteration to Pompeyo's wife. My focus then became getting my family out of Cuba.

I communicated with Cirilo, one of Willy's brothers who lived in the United States. He said he was doing everything he could to move the process forward.

Each family who had applied to leave Cuba had been assigned a nucleus number. Every night, I listened to the Spanish-language transmissions from a Miami radio station and waited until the announcer revealed the numbers of the latest families arriving in the United States. My eyes glistened as I heard the words that followed: "We would like to welcome all the families to the land of the free. Welcome to the United States of America."

Perhaps these weren't the exact words, as so many years have passed, but chills ran through me when I heard them. I remember keeping the volume of the radio very low because if any neighbors heard me listening to a prohibited radio station, my life could have become more complicated than it already was.

With everything going on in my life, I had neglected to see what was happening with my sister. That was until one day when, after she finished school, we received the visit of a young man.

Nancy sat in one of the rocking chairs, and he in the other looking at her with a nervous expression. I asked Phil to go play in my room, and he stomped his feet and gave the young man an angry look. He then took his red truck and walked away.

"Ms. Madeline, I wanted to talk to you about Nancy and me," he said. He glanced at my sister again, and she smiled shyly, tucking her long hair behind her ear. "It's important you know that we love each other very much. I would like your permission to date her until our marriage. I want to marry her as soon as possible."

I had to keep from laughing when I saw these two children discussing marriage. It was probably the same way my father felt when Willy came to our house for the first time. Alexis, Nancy's boyfriend, was an affable, tall young man, as skinny as sugarcane. Nancy and he made a handsome couple, but I now understood there was so much more to a successful relationship than love.

"How old are you?" I asked.

"Seventeen, miss, but I'll be eighteen in six months."

"Do you know how old Nancy is?"

"Yes. She will be seventeen in eight months."

"So, she's sixteen, right?"

"Yes, miss."

"Do you see where I'm going with this?"

"Are you saying she's too young, miss? I can assure you that she's very mature. All we want is to be with each other."

"I do love him, Madeline," Nancy said.

I took a deep breath.

"You understand this is something I can't approve. You will have to speak to our parents."

"But, if you help us, Sister, that conversation will be easier," replied Nancy.

I remained quiet for a moment.

"Please, Made," said Nancy. "I have never asked you for anything in my life. However, I've always defended you since I was a little girl. Help me please."

"There's so much going on, Nancy, and you know what our goal is."

"You mean, leaving Cuba, miss?" Alexis said.

I crossed my arms and stared at Nancy.

"I'm not as stupid as I look, miss. I know your husband was taken away because you're leaving Cuba. Nancy didn't have to tell me anything. Besides, I will always do what I think is best for her. I'm prepared to work hard."

At the time, I failed to understand that response and convinced myself that Alexis shared my beliefs when the opposite was true.

"What do you do for a living?" I asked.

"I'm a carpenter, a good one, but I also go to school."

"Where will you live if the two of you get married?"

"I'm building a small house," he said.

141

Chapter 23 - Nancy

I took a deep breath and glanced at my sister. I asked him many more questions, and each reply satisfied me. At the end of my interrogation, Nancy asked: "Will you help us?"

"If this is what you want... I will talk to our parents next time they visit."

She rose from her chair and gave me a hug. Alexis thanked me.

"Can I visit Nancy, miss?"

"You can come on Saturdays. During the week, she must focus on her studies."

Between my sewing responsibilities, my son, and my constant worrying, I could not endure chaperoning my sister more than once a week. Nancy seemed disappointed and, having experienced the pain of being away from the man I loved, I understood her frustration.

After he left, Nancy said she had homework to do and left me in the living room alone. It was a hot July day, and unlike other days, I kept my windows closed. I didn't want to listen to the neighbors or to the children play. I didn't want to listen to the happiness of others.

I looked at a picture of Willy and me on the wall, taken on the day of our wedding, the only picture I had of that day. Then I realized I had to go back to my sewing.

If Nancy only knew how hard life could be, the complexities of a marriage, the responsibilities of a wife, she would not be jumping into it so quickly, but she had inherited my hard headedness. I saw how she looked at

Alexis, the same way I looked at Willy when I was her age.

Chapter 24 – The Secret

Narrator: Madeline

I kept tossing and turning, unable to sleep, sensing something was wrong. I knew my parents were fine. I had seen them a couple of days before when I told them about Nancy and her boyfriend. My father seemed disappointed, but not as much as when Willy told him we were in love. Maybe now he had expected it. He knew the day would come when he would lose her too. Besides, the two of them never had the opportunity to get as close as he and I had become.

Nancy was my mother's baby, her pride and joy. During most of Nancy formative years, Dad had become more distant and introspective. The revolution changed him. So, Nancy never knew the version of my father I was fortunate to know during the happiest times of his life.

After Alexis spoke to my father, Papá thought about taking Nancy to my grandfather's house for a while, but Nancy began to weep and embraced my mother, knowing she would do anything to help her.

Chapter 24 – The Secret

"Don't let Dad take me away from Alexis, Mom," Nancy cried with the dramaturgical skills of an experienced actress, reminding me of my mother. I had enough drama in my life to have to deal with a spoiled teenager. However, Nancy had no option but to stay with me. Besides, the entire educational system had changed. Children had to attend government schools, and those close to where I lived were better than the school in the countryside.

After much discussion, Nancy agreed to stay at the farm with my parents for two weeks during part of the summer break. If at the end of those two weeks, she still felt the same way, my father would think about allowing her to date Alexis. I felt relieved. That would give me time to adapt to the idea of being the chaperone to my baby sister. Until then, Nancy had not been a difficult child. It had been a pleasure to live with her, but that was about to change.

As agreed, Nancy packed a bag and left. After her departure, the house felt empty. That night, unable to sleep, I got out of bed and went to the living room. I wondered whether I should read or keep working. In the end, I turned on the radio and raised the volume just enough to listen to the Miami radio station.

I lost track of time and dozed off, only to be awakened by loud knocking on the door and the sound of a male voice calling my name. After I rubbed my eyes, I heard the voice again. It sounded familiar, but it couldn't be who I was thinking.

Chapter 24 – The Secret

When I opened the door and saw him, I couldn't believe it was him. His eyes looked sunken. His muscles had disappeared, and he had a skeletal thinness. However, I recognized his smile.

"Willy?" I said. "Dear God! Is it you?"

He nodded and we embraced, but I felt as if I was embracing someone else. I let him in, closed the door, and we cried in each other's arms for a while, telling each other how difficult life had been without the other.

"Are you staying for good?"

"No," he said. "I'm sick. I'm only here a few days to recover."

"What did they do to you?"

"Lack of food and parasites. They were giving us water contaminated with latrine waste."

"Those animals."

I grabbed him by a hand and led him to our bedroom to help him out of his filthy clothes.

"Where's our son?" he said.

"Asleep. Take a shower and eat first. I'll wake him up after you're done."

Later, when I woke up little Phil, and he saw his father's face, his eyes glowed with a joy I had not seen since Willy left. His little arms reached over his father's neck while his dad lifted him out of bed and embraced him.

"My little man!" Willy said. "Look how much you've grown in the last few months. Taking care of your mom?"

Chapter 24 – The Secret

Phil nodded. Willy's eyes filled with tears as he caressed his son's black hair. My husband then thanked me for caring for Phil and waiting for him to return.

"When I leave again, I don't know how long it will be before I am able to return," he said in an apologetic tone.

"My love, I'll wait for you for the rest of my life. Nothing will change that."

He didn't respond, but he looked at me with a shine in his eyes that I knew too well. He didn't have to say anything.

We spent the rest of the evening making up for lost time. Phil showed him the letters of the alphabet and colors he had learned, while I enjoyed watching the two most important people in my life interacting with each other. I knew that soon we would have to say goodbye once again. I consoled myself with the idea I would have him for a few days. For the next two days, I pampered him and took time away from my sewing to cater to his every need.

I wasn't expecting it when, on the third day, officers came to the house to ask Willy to report to the authorities.

As difficult as it was to see Willy leave the first time, the second felt far worse as I now feared for his life. Before he left, I embraced him, thinking it might be the last time.

"*Papi*, I want you to stay home," Phil said, looking up at his father and holding his hand.

Willy lifted him and kissed his head.

"Take care of mami, okay?"

Phil nodded.

After Willy walked out wearing a clean shirt and pants that looked too big on him, I sat on a chair and wept. My three-year-old stood in front of me, touched my face, and kept asking me to stop.

I started to call Cirilo almost daily, begging him to accelerate the process, explaining that it was a matter of life and death. Cirilo assured me he was doing everything he could. He said it would not be much longer.

Luis, the man who delivered the departure notices in our neighborhood must have heard about my desperation because one night, after my son went to bed, he came to my house. I didn't open the door at first.

"What do you need?" I asked without opening.

"I bring news from your husband."

I unlocked the door and let him in. After he sat in one of the rocking chairs, I offered him coffee. Once I brought it, Luis revealed the true purpose of his visit.

"I could help you, Madeline," the middle-aged man said, taking a sip of the steamy liquid. "You're young and very beautiful. I would be discrete, of course. It would be a transaction between two consenting adults. No one needs to find out."

I could feel the blood rushing to my head. Unwilling to listen to his nonsense, I got up and pointed towards the door.

"Get out of my house!" I yelled.

148

Chapter 24 – The Secret

"You don't have to get upset, *mi amor*," he said, handing me his cup. I took it and threw against the concrete floor, causing the ceramic cup to shatter into tiny pieces. I had never acted like this. It wasn't in my nature. Yet, when he threatened what I held dear, when he tried to compromise my sense of decency, something inside me snapped.

"Get out of my house, and I don't ever want to see you again, not until my husband is safe at home, and you bring us a notice that we can leave."

"That won't happen without other preconditions."

Ignoring him, I dashed towards the door, opened it and pointed towards the street with my index finger.

"Out!"

Luis laughed and walked out slowly, touching my face with his fingers.

"Feisty! The way I like it," he said. The moment he stepped outside, I shut the door in his face and sat on a chair in the living room to cry.

After I calmed down, I decided not to tell anyone about this encounter. If Willy learned about what happened, I was certain he would confront him after his release. The last thing I wanted was a fight that could only end with Willy in jail for years or dead. I couldn't say a word to anyone. That would the first secret I kept from my husband.

Chapter 25 - Waiting

Narrator: Madeline

Nancy stood in front of a mirror applying a crimson color to her full lips while I looked at her with pride. My little sister had grown into a beautiful woman, and I couldn't believe she was about to become a wife. She still referred to me as her second mom, except that now she and I were the same height. Unlike me, who often kept thoughts to myself, Nancy spoke her mind, but not in ways that others found offensive, just the opposite. Even when she delivered bad news, she managed to remain charming.

"What do you think?" she asked, turning around to look at me.

"Simply gorgeous, the most beautiful bride I've ever seen."

My words made her smile, and she hugged me and thanked me for making her wedding dress.

"You're the best sister in the world," she said.

I escorted her to the courtyard where the rest of the family awaited, and the ceremony began. Held at the house of her groom's parents, it was attended by some of her closest friends and our parents—who still lived at my grandparents' farm, about an hour from Arroyo Blanco. By then, Arroyo Blanco had become a ghost of what it had been. Many people had abandoned it, some to move to other cities in search of jobs, others to go abroad to start a new life.

For the ceremony, Nancy wore a white veil and a simple white dress that reached down to her knees. The couple didn't have a religious service as the new government frowned upon the practice of religion. When the justice of the peace declared the couple husband and wife, I saw on the faces of the newlyweds the joy that Willy and I had at our wedding. They belonged together.

He had built her a small house behind his parents' home. Nothing fancy, just a couple of bedrooms, a tiny kitchen, and a small living room, dining room, and bathroom. Their house was unfinished but livable. He had built a cement sink, which he painted green, and bought her a Russian washer that washed but didn't rinse.

For the reception, his family used their connections to purchase a pig, so we ate roast pork, rice, beans, and a piece of cake. At the end of the reception, a friend picked them up in his car to take them to their hotel.

Willy couldn't attend the wedding as he was still away doing forced labor. I prayed that

Chapter 25 - Waiting

Nancy and her husband never experienced the months of separation Willy and I had.

After Nancy's wedding, her mother-in-law began to give her special herbs to stop her from getting pregnant. She thought Nancy and her husband Alexis were too young to have children. I feared that all those home remedies would affect her ability to have children in the future and asked her not to take them, but Nancy didn't want to upset her mother-in-law. It was the only time she refrained from telling someone how she felt. That told me just how much she loved her husband.

Phil liked visiting Lala, Nancy's mother-in-law, because she had chickens, cows, and a daughter who was his age. A couple of times, when he and the little girl went into the open barn to play, Phil stole eggs from the chickens, cracked them, and ate them raw. I felt so embarrassed.

"Why would you do that?" I asked, crossing my arms over my head.

Lala laughed. She said that the egg yolks, which had a reddish color, were the healthiest food he could eat because of the natural foods her chickens ate.

Lala pitied my son. It saddened her to see him growing up without his father. To supplement the half-liter of milk to which he was entitled via the ration card, she began to send him milk from her cows. Nancy and I thanked her for her kindness, but it felt uncomfortable to accept the milk. I asked Nancy if I should at least pay for it. Nancy said that would offend her, so I desisted.

Once Nancy began the new stage of her life, I refocused my energies on leaving Cuba, pressing Cirilo to help us before it was too late. At Willy's request, I had not visited him for several months. The government had moved him to a more remote area not accessible by bus. In his letters, sent with friends, he told me he had lost over 70 pounds. I wasn't sure how much longer he could withstand the living conditions. Cirilo would tell me it was only a matter of time.

It had been almost two years since Willy left home. Afraid my son would forget his father, I showed him pictures of him often.

"I don't like the police," he would tell me. "They took my dad."

The drawings of our four-year-old had become bolder, more violent. They materialized the anger I carried inside.

The boy's brightness surprised everyone. He already knew how to write, and I was teaching him how to add and subtract. My time alone had been devoted to him and my sewing, which allowed us to bond in a special way.

By then, my friend Mirta had gotten married, not to the young man she had dated when I lived in Arroyo Blanco, but to an older man. Although time and distance erased our friendship, I heard she was happy.

I missed Tía Rita. My father told me that the time she had spent away from her husband tested the strength of her marriage. Yet, despite facing infidelities and illnesses, she hid her sadness behind her smile until the day of her death.

Willy's parents and most of his brothers and sisters had already left Cuba. Some went to Port Chester, New York, but Cirilo had stayed in New York City. Through letters, Willy's brothers would tell me about life in the United States. Their first winter had been exciting. They had seen snow for the first time and could not say enough about it, from the snowman they made at the Jose Martí Park in Port Chester, to the chains they had to install on their tires when a thick blanket of snow covered the streets.

Port Chester was a small town inhabited by an eclectic population: German, Italian, Polish, and Cuban primarily. Willy's family had fallen in love with the place since they arrived, and I could not wait until we joined them.

Lined with white two-story houses, duplexes mostly, that had aluminum siding and shingle roofs, the town enjoyed an envious geographical location. Its railroad track allowed it access to New York City via a forty-minute ride by train.

I pictured Willy, little Phil, my parents, my sister, and her husband sitting around a large table at a house in Port Chester. I imagined my son playing in the snow.

Despite the distance from their place of birth, none of Willy's brothers had abandoned their traditions. If anything, they strengthened them by getting together during birthday celebrations, playing Cuban music, and cooking big meals that were becoming more Americanized as time passed. I could imagine such a life, but it seemed so distant.

Every night, I listened to the numbers of families arriving in the United States. Ours was getting closer.

Chapter 26 – The Return

Narrator: Madeline

I don't know how I went from being infatuated with my husband to being so in love with him that the notion of being away from him hurt me on an emotional and physical level. During the first few days following his departure, I would look out the window, hoping for his return, but as the days turned into months, and hope into disappointment, I stopped glancing at the streets.

Forty-five days had passed with no word from my husband, and I was worried. I stayed as busy as I could, the only way I knew to keep my sanity. When I didn't have anything to do, or at night, when silence accompanied me, my thoughts returned, sinking me into despair.

One sunny afternoon, as I stood in the kitchen cooking yellow rice and chicken, I heard someone knocking. I washed my hands and walked towards the door, passing by my son, who sat on the floor of the living room playing with his red truck.

I opened the door slowly, noticing first the sunken cheeks, a paleness that terrified me, the thin arms, like those of men who had been in Germany's concentration camps. I recognized his small eyes!

"What did they do to you?" I said, embracing him and kissing him on the cheeks dozens of times, my eyes full of tears.

"Mami, who's there?" my son asked.

I opened the door wide to let Willy in. When my son saw his father and me holding hands, he rose from the floor and walked towards him with uncertainty.

"Papi?"

"Yes, son. It's me."

Phil ran to him. As weak as Willy looked, he picked up Phil, and father and son embraced while I hugged them both.

"Oh, sweetheart, what have they done to you?" I asked again.

My husband was a shadow of the man I had married.

He put Phil on the floor, as if realizing how dirty he was.

"Can I shower and get something to eat first?"

Of course. What was I thinking? I rushed to the kitchen, and he went to the bathroom to shower. When he finished, I served him a big plate of steamy yellow rice and chicken. He asked me for an empty plate to remove half of what I had given him. He said it was too much food. While the three of us sat around the dining room table, I asked him again what had happened to him.

"They hardly fed us and cooked what they gave us with contaminated water. I have parasites."

I shook my head.

"I want to kill those men, Papi," my four-year-old son said, closing his fists.

"You're not killing anyone, son. There is a God, and those men will pay for what they've done."

I didn't know if I believed my husband's words, but I knew we needed to leave Cuba as soon as possible.

"Do you have to go back?" I asked.

"No. I still have to work for them, but they will allow me to sleep at home."

My husband sounded like a broken man. He had lost his drive and the intensity of his gaze.

"I can't wait for the moment when all of us, Nancy and her husband, my parents, and the three of us say goodbye to this God-forsaken country. All I want is to see us in Port Chester with the rest of the family."

"Nancy got married?"

I nodded.

He asked me about her husband. I told him she was as lucky as I was to have found a good man.

"I wish they could leave at the same time as us, but they will have to wait," I said.

"Why?"

"Cirilo only claimed her. The papers need to be revised, and that takes time."

Chapter 26 – The Return

That night, when we went to bed, I wept in silence after my husband made love to me. He felt like a different man, but I promised myself to nurse him back to health. If I loved him before he left, my love for him had evolved into something different and stronger. The men who took him thought they would destroy us, but instead, we became more committed to each other.

Before we fell asleep in each other's arms, he whispered in my ear, "I thought I would die before seeing you again. Only the idea of kissing your lips and having you in my arms again kept me alive. Now I can die happy."

"I won't let you die. I want my husband to be by my side for the rest of my days. I love you."

"I love you my beautiful girl from Arroyo Blanco. Now more than ever."

Chapter 27 – Luis's Visit

Narrator: Madeline

When I answered the door, Luis's presence in front of me caused me to clinch my fists. Before I could ask him what he wanted, he pushed the door wide open and walked in. Dressed in his olive-green military uniform, with an air of self-importance that accompanied each of his rigid steps, he said:

"I have orders to take an inventory of your personal belongings."

Judging by the way he raised his chin and looked down at me, he seemed pleased to have been assigned this task. My son stopped playing with his red truck and gave him a serious look.

Willy was home. He had stopped by to have lunch and freshen up before returning to his new duties at a construction site. Having him at home made me feel thankful but nervous. Afraid he would notice my unwelcoming glances towards Luis, I told Willy I would stay in the kitchen washing the dishes while Luis took the inventory, but other thoughts occupied my mind. The fact that Luis was taking an inventory meant that our departure date was approaching.

In a few days, I would no longer be able to cook in the tiny kitchen where I had prepared so many meals for my family. I inspected my surroundings in silence: the small gas stove of two burners, the tiny countertops on either side. My husband had installed a cabinet on an adjacent wall. Nothing fancy. Two doors and enough space for some spices and a few groceries. I wondered who would cook in this kitchen, who would take over my things.

This inventory conveyed the beginning of the end.

The thought of a stranger inventorying my belongings made me ill, but I knew those were the rules. The government would keep all my possessions. This was the price we had to pay for leaving Cuba.

Luis made a detailed list as he went through the house. Willy later told me that he even counted the sheets, the furniture, and detailed the contents of each drawer. He also wrote down the brand of our mattress. When he made it to the kitchen, I excused myself and went to the living room, evading his eyes as I passed by him.

Willy followed me. "Is everything okay?"

I nodded. "I don't like people looking through my stuff," I whispered.

My husband stared at me, as if trying to interpret what I was thinking. He then joined Luis to make sure he didn't steal anything, as if it mattered.

I remained nervous until Luis left the house. At that moment, I looked at my husband and shrugged my shoulders.

"Now we wait," I said.

He smiled.

Over the course of the next two weeks, Cirilo sent me a couple of telegrams with the same message.

"Be on alert. You'll receive your documents any time now."

I didn't know how quickly the process would move. All we could do was wait.

My sister came to visit me every afternoon. She loved to talk and share every detail of her life with me. One of those afternoons, she said, "I love my life. I love my husband, and my in-laws. And guess what? I have a surprise for you. You're going to die when you hear it!"

I glanced at her with inquisitive eyes, noticing she had not lost the innocence of her childhood. I could still imagine her telling me "defend yourself, Madeline," like she had done so many times through the years, when she thought I had allowed my mother to step all over me.

Just when she was about to tell me her surprise, we heard someone knock. I opened and saw Luis. "I'm back!" he said. Consistent with his last visit, Luis pushed my door open, except that this time, he handed me some papers before he entered.

"Those are your departure documents," he said. "You need to leave in two days."

162

Chapter 27 – Luis's Visit

I glanced at my sister, who now stood in the living room looking at me.

"I need to check that everything on the inventory is still here. If something is missing, you won't be able to leave. You hear me?"

The sound of his voice angered me. Until the day I met him, I had never felt hatred. It was an unsettling, all-consuming feeling that eroded my insides. In my mind, Luis represented everything that was wrong with the revolution.

In his hand, Luis held a piece of paper with handwriting on both sides. He walked past my sister as if he owned the house, ignoring her and checking off items on his list. "While I'm doing this, can I get some coffee?"

I gave him an empty glance, but my sister took control of the situation.

"Of course, comrade. Let me bring you a cup. It would be my pleasure."

My sister went to the kitchen, and while Luis surveyed my bedroom's contents, I grabbed a roll of fabric I had hidden inside a cabinet in the dining room and placed it under my arm. Thinking we had plenty of time, my mother had brought it to me a day after the initial inventory was finished and asked me to make a set of pajamas for Phil. Neither one of us knew the rules or realized we could take very little out of Cuba. Regardless, I didn't have time to make it.

I placed the fabric under my arm and tiptoed out of the house through the side door next to the dining room. Carlota lived in the house next to mine, so I threw the fabric over to her yard. At the time, she was sitting in a rocking chair on her porch. As one of my few friends in the neighborhood, she knew I would leave soon. The moment she saw me throw the fabric, she rushed outside, picked it up, and looked at me with an inquisitive glance. I placed my index finger perpendicular to my lips. As if realizing what was going on, she took the fabric inside.

A couple of weeks earlier, Carlota, a mother of three, had asked me for my wedding ring because she and her husband could not afford one. I gave it to her, as I knew that Luis had not seen my ring during his inventory visit.

During this visit, Luis spent about thirty minutes at my house, including the time it took him to drink the coffee. Before leaving, he stared at me with distrust.

"Nothing on this list can be removed. If it is, you won't be able to leave. Understood?"

I couldn't get myself to respond and looked the other way.

"Yes, officer. Don't worry. My sister understands the rules, and nothing will be touched," said Nancy in a cheerful voice.

Luis ignored her and gave me an intense stare.

"I'll be back in about an hour to close the house. You need to be ready to vacate the premises by then. You, your husband, and your kid can take a piece of luggage with a change of clothes. That's all. Everything else has to stay."

Luis left, and Nancy and I began to pack, while Carlota offered to go to Willy's job and ask him to rush home. After we were done, Nancy remained quiet as I walked around my house one last time.

I sat on a chair in the dining room, watching my son play, wishing I had his innocence. Our lives were about to change, but my son could only focus on his favorite toy, a truck he rode in the air through invisible streets, while he made engine noises.

I felt Nancy's hands on my shoulder and her lips on my face as she gave me a kiss. "I'll miss my big sister and my nephew so much. Don't forget about me, you hear?"

Her voice was sweet, like the *guarapo* my grandparents' workers made from sugarcane while I was growing up.

She sat by my side and joined me in my silence, watching my wandering eyes as they recorded every corner of the place that had been my home.

All my furniture, a porcelain horse that adorned my coffee table—which was a gift from my father—and the family pictures on the walls had to stay. I tried to carve those last moments at my house in my mind, thinking nothing would ever be as it was.

By the time Luis returned, we were locking the door. I handed him the key without looking at him and grabbed my son by the hand.

"Hey!" he yelled. "Why are you taking that toy?"

I noticed the little red truck in the hands of my four-year-old.

"That truck has to stay," he said.

My son glanced at me and then at Luis.

"This is my truck!" Phil yelled. "It's not yours." Little Phil held the truck against his chest, but with a quick maneuver, Luis grabbed it away from him. Phil started to hit Luis with his small fists.

"Get away from me, you little *mocoso*," Luis yelled, pushing my son. The boy lost his balance and fell on the sidewalk.

"I want my truck back!" he began to cry. "Give me my truck. It's mine!"

Nancy took the two pieces of luggage I was carrying, one strapped around my shoulder and the other in my hand, and I picked up my son from the sidewalk and carried him in my arms. Phil kicked and screamed for his toy.

"You don't need it, son. Soon, I'll buy a new one. He can keep that one."

I kissed him and caressed him on the way to Lala's house, but he was inconsolable. After a while, his screams turned into silent weeping.

After I arrived at Lala's house, I realized I needed to get a message to my parents about my trip. One of Alexis's relatives offered to pick them up and bring them to Lala's house, as she had more space than Alexis did. That would allow me to spend some time with them before we left.

Chapter 27 – Luis's Visit

While we waited for my parents to arrive, Nancy asked me to leave Phil with Alexis at his parents' house while I accompanied her to hers. She wanted a quiet place to talk.

Once we entered Nancy's house, we each sat on one of her dining room chairs. She grabbed my hand, caressed it, and smiled.

"I know that you're leaving in two days, and that the time may not be perfect, but I wanted to tell you this myself. You know how much I love Alexis. Sharing my life with him is the best thing that has happened to me, and only what I am about to tell you could make me as happy."

"Tell me once and for all. No need to be so mysterious."

"My sister, in a few months, you will be an aunt. I'm pregnant!" she said.

"You're what?" I asked in shock.

"Isn't that wonderful?" she said touching her belly.

"But... I thought you were coming with us to the United States."

"We'll figure things out later. Stop worrying about everything. Life is too short to live that way."

I shook my head.

"Adding the baby will take more time," I said.

"If things don't work out, you can always visit us. It's not like you are going to the other side of the world."

I gave her a perplexed look and kept my thoughts to myself. I didn't want to upset her.

Chapter 27 – Luis's Visit

When my parents arrived, Dad glanced at me with a sad look. As much as he had wanted me to leave Cuba, now that the moment neared, his reaction was not what I had expected.

"Two days?" he asked, as if hoping it wasn't true.

"Yes, Dad."

"So, I guess this is it."

"We'll see each other again, soon," I said. He looked at me with a serious expression.

"My little Phil" my mother said kissing my son on his cheeks. "I'm going to miss you so much."

She embraced him in her usual melodramatic way.

"Madeline, on the day of your flight, I'll go with you to the airport," she said. "But your father will stay here. It will be too much for his health."

I glanced at my father. "Papá, are you okay?"

"Your mother is being too protective, as usual. I'm fine."

"You're staying with Nancy, and that's final," my mother said.

He waived his hand in dismissal but didn't argue with her.

The night before we left, we were all invited to the house of Alexis's parents for a big meal. There wasn't enough space at the dining table for everyone, so Lala borrowed Alexis's table and placed it in her living room. Lala outdid herself that night. Black beans, rice, chicken, even a flan. Throughout the course of the meal, Mamá and Lala did most of the talking, while Papá remained reserved and pensive.

"Take a lot of pictures, my little sister-in-law," Alexis said with a big smile. He took a spoonful of black beans, and once he devoured it, he added, "And don't forget about the hungry people of Cuba."

Nancy hit him on his arm with a closed fist and said, "Stop that! You're not hungry."

"But if my mami didn't have this land, I would be very hungry. Besides, that's between Madeline and me. Stop spoiling our deal."

We all laughed.

After dinner, Phil went to play with the chickens in the backyard. I reminded him to not take their eggs. Instead of acknowledging my request, he stared at me and walked out.

Mamá and my sister helped Lala retire the empty plates from the table. I tried to help, but Lala insisted I was the guest of honor and should relax, so I invited my father to come to the porch with me instead. We sat in rocking chairs next to each other, looking at the dirt road in front of us.

"Only a few hours left," he said.

I grabbed his hand. "Yes, Papá... I'll miss you."

He nodded. "I know you will."

"I'll get you out of Cuba next, Papá."

His eyes focused on the floor. "Your mother won't leave until Nancy leaves, and now Nancy's pregnant." He took a deep breath.

169

"We'll figure something out, Papá. I promise."

Chapter 28 – Leaving Camagüey

Narrator: Madeline

Around five, Pepe, the driver to whom we had paid six-hundred pesos for the round trip between Ciudad de Camagüey and Varadero, arrived in his old Chevrolet to pick up Willy, Phil, my mother, my neighbor Carlota, and me. Carlota sat in the front and the rest of us in the back. Willy and I held hands, and little Phil sat between his grandmother and me, his head leaning against my shoulder as he slept.

After a short drive, we began to go west on the Carretera Central, an east-west highway that spanned the length of the island. Our destination, the beach town of Varadero, was in the Province of Matanzas.

We remained quiet for a while to avoid waking Phil. We had decided not to tell him where we were going. What was the point? I wondered how long it would take before he figured it out.

At first, we didn't know if the driver had connections to the government, a reason not to have any sensitive conversations around him. He came highly recommended, but we could not afford to trust anyone.

Chapter 28 – Leaving Camagüey

"So why are you leaving?" he asked after a while.

"We want to join my brothers and my parents," Willy said, looking at little Phil.

"Not only that, but to have a good life," the driver said. "I hear that the United States is the land of opportunity."

"The United States?" Phil asked with his eyes half-closed. "Where is that?"

"It's a place for vacations," I said.

"I like vacations," he replied and went back to sleep.

Carlota touched Pepe's arm, placed her finger across her lips, and whispered something in his ear. He apologized for mentioning the United States but continued to ask questions. We responded with half-answers and smiles.

I was nervous. We had to get to our destination before five, and the car was old and smelled like gasoline. We traveled with our windows down because it didn't have an air-conditioner, so inside, the air felt humid and warm.

It was Saturday, October 19, 1969. During this month, the temperatures in these parts remained at a more tolerable level than in August, when a journey like this would've been unbearable.

Our four-year-old slept until the first glimpses of sun appeared. Then, he stretched his little arms, and his eyes focused outside the car with curiosity.

Chapter 28 – Leaving Camagüey

"Where are we going?" Phil asked as if he had forgotten his earlier question when he was half-asleep.

"On vacation," his father said.

"Is abuelita coming?"

"No, but we won't be gone for too long."

It was the first time either one of us had left the Province of Camagüey. Wide-eyed, Phil pointed at the forests, the stretches of luscious plains adorned by tall queen palm trees and the small houses with thatched roofs scattered along the way. He asked many questions, always curious, always trying to expand his knowledge about his surroundings.

The separation from his father matured him beyond his years, and when all the sudden, my mother began to cry, he turned to her and asked, "Abuelita, why are you crying? Papá said we won't be gone for too long. We'll see you again soon."

His grandmother caressed his head and exchanged glances with me, as thoughts kept betraying me, telling me something would happen that would deter our plan. Then fear took hold of me, the same fear I experienced as a child.

In some stretches of the road, the forests' thickness and canopied trees would make it appear as if we were driving inside a tunnel, and for a moment, I marveled at our surroundings. Then, I would once again consult Willy's wristwatch, afraid we wouldn't make it on time. Not even the animated conversation between Carlota and our driver could take my mind away from my ominous thoughts.

A few hours passed, and just when I had convinced myself that I had been overthinking, I heard a popping noise. At first, I didn't know what had caused it, so my eyes focused on the driver. In an instant, Pepe traded the jokes and light conversation by cussing, followed by: "That's all I needed. I can't believe this keeps happening to me!"

Pepe stopped on the side of the road and exited the car. We watched from inside as he inspected it. He then placed his arms up in the air, as if realizing what had happened. He screamed obscenities, stamped his feet, and when he noticed our disapproving glances, he apologized.

Willy got out of the car to help him. Pepe opened the trunk of the car, retrieved a used spare tire, and used a jack to raise the car and remove the flat. Thirty minutes later, our journey continued.

Around two, Pepe announced we would be at our hotel in less than two hours, but the pessimist in me wasn't convinced. When another tire popped an hour later and Pepe almost lost control of the car, I whispered to Willy, "Oh my God, we're are not going to make it!"

My mother must have heard me. By then, Pepe had managed to park the car by the side of the road, and there we were, in the middle of nowhere.

"You knew that my daughter needed to arrive on time!" Mamá yelled at Pepe. "How dare you risk my family like this when you knew your car wasn't safe? Are you crazy?"

Pepe slammed the steering wheel with his closed fists, as if he had lost his mind. He also said words that a decent woman should not repeat, and for his sake, I was glad that my father wasn't around to hear them.

"Pepe, watch your language," Willy said.

"I'm sorry. I knew my tires were bad, but it's hard to find a replacement. I'm sorry."

Filled with panic, I thought we would have to return home. But, what home? I started to feel light-headed when Pepe announced: "We have to walk. A friend of mine has a shop only a couple of kilometers away. He owns a car."

"Under this heat? Are you insane?" my mother shouted.

The driver waived his hands in the air.

"Señora, what do you want me to do? My tires were old. I thought I would be able to make it. I'm sorry."

Realizing that arguing would not fix our problem, we got out of the car and began to walk on the grassy field by the side of the road. I was on the verge of tears as I noticed the time on Willy's watch. *We were not going to make it!* While we walked, Phil dragged his feet and lifted dirt with his shoes.

"Stop, or you'll ruin your shoes," his father said. Willy picked up Phil and placed him over his shoulder. Beads of sweat gathered on

Phil's head. As much as he enjoyed running after butterflies, after seeing several fly by, it surprised me he didn't ask his father to put him down so he could run after them. Perhaps, he was too tired from the long trip.

Willy carried him for a little while until I asked him to let me do it, as Willy had hardly gained five pounds since his return from the fields and was still weak.

My mother's complaining continued, making our journey more frustrating. On either side of the road, grass and trees as far as the eye could see dominated the landscape, brightened by sunlight and contrasting the cloudless blue skies. Before long, my blouse was sticking to my sweaty back.

"We'll never get there! Oh my God. I can't believe this is happening," my mother kept repeating, not using the exact same words each time but conveying the same message.

Willy kept shaking his head and staring at her. She ignored him. After a while, he approached her and whispered something in her ear that I couldn't decipher. Although didn't say a word the rest of the way, with the angry glances she kept giving Willy, words were unnecessary.

While we walked, a set of unexpected events were unfolding in Camagüey.

The news of my departure had spread through the town where I lived, and while men worked and women cooked dinner for their families, someone broke into my house. Nancy didn't find out until the next morning, when the officer who had taken the inventory showed up at her house and asked where I was. She explained we had left the day before. "I will notify the authorities right now. They can't leave. I told you that if anything was taken out of the house, they would not be able to leave," Luis said.

"But we haven't taken anything."

"You probably told the person who broke in."

"I would never do that!"

Nancy tried to reason with him and invited him to a cup of coffee, but nothing could persuade him. My father was staying with her while Mamá traveled with me to Matanzas. At the time, he was reading in the backyard. Afraid my father would hear the argument, Nancy kept looking towards the back, while Luis kept raising his voice.

"I'm going to inspect your house right now! If I find anything that belongs to your sister here, you and your husband are going to jail!" Luis yelled.

She opened the door and let him in, noticing the anger in his eyes as he went through her belongings. He opened every drawer and threw things on the floor. Nancy caressed her belly thinking of the baby growing inside her, wondering if Luis would make up an excuse to take her and Alexis to jail anyway.

"They won't be able to get away with it!" he yelled on the way out, pointing at her with his index finger.

Chapter 29 – Saying Goodbye

Narrator: Madeline

We had abandoned the Carretera Central and walked on a narrow two-way street in the town of Varadero. An hour had passed since we left our car on the side of the road. Drenched in sweat and having drank all the water we brought with us, we hoped to refill the bottles upon our arrival at the shop.

We arrived after three, exhausted.

The gas station—old, run-down, with rotting tires tossed around—had a single pump. The attendant came out to greet us wearing clothes that were soiled from dirt and engine grease. His smile broadened as he approached us, wiping his hands with a rag.

After greeting us, Pepe followed him to the back of the shop, leaving us in the reception area.

"We won't get there on time," I whispered to Willy.

"That's what I said before," my mother replied, staring at Willy with her eyebrows raised.

Chapter 29 – Saying Goodbye

"Let me see what's going on," Willy said and walked towards the back of the shop holding in his hand a bag with empty bottles. Meanwhile, Mamá caressed little Phil's hair, a pensive look on her face.

"Everything will be fine," Carlota said, as if noticing my mother's preoccupation.

I wasn't so sure.

Moments later, Willy returned.

"A guy called Fernando is coming to pick us up," Willy said and began to distribute the full bottles of water. "He's a friend of the guy who works at the shop. Fernando owns a car and will take us to our hotel."

Thirty minutes later, a white-haired man driving an old blue car arrived. We all looked at each other.

"Is that *the* car?" my mother asked.

"Don't worry, señora," said Fernando. "As old as this car looks, it is in great shape."

Our previous driver would not be able to return my mother and our neighbor to Camagüey as it would take a couple of days before the replacement tire arrived. Therefore, he refunded half of the money to my husband, who gave it to Fernando.

Twenty minutes before the deadline, we arrived at the hotel, hoping to get some rest. Once we paid the front desk for a night's stay, the clerk said, "You can go up to your room for only a few minutes. I'm calling a taxi now that will take you to an undisclosed location. Although you are required to pay for one night, you won't stay here, so bring your luggage down. You will need to take it with you to the processing center."

We thanked the clerk and walked to a side of the lobby where my mother and Carlota could sit to wait for us. Willy and I opened the pieces of luggage and gathered what we planned to wear in one of them. We left two of the pieces with my mother and Carlota, and Willy carried the one with our clothes to the room, while I held Phil in my arms. Afraid to miss our taxi, we quickly washed our faces and armpits, changed our sweaty clothes, and returned to the lobby to say our goodbyes.

"Well, Mamá," I said after leaving Phil with Willy and standing in front of my mother. "It's time to go."

"I know," she said looking at me with tenderness and caressing my face. "Madi, I know we haven't had the best relationship through the years. I'll miss you very much and won't rest until we see each other again, you hear? Take care of my grandson. He's my life."

"I know, mami," I said trying to hold back the tears.

I felt a hand on my shoulder.

"Madeline, the taxi is here," Willy said.

"Give your Grandma a hug, Phil," I said

I put him Willy down, and he rushed to his grandmother and embraced her legs.

"I'll see you soon," my mother said, bending over to kiss his face. "Take care of your mom, okay?"

Phil nodded and looked around as if he didn't understand what was about to happen.

180

Chapter 29 – Saying Goodbye

Willy embraced my mother and our neighbor, and we rushed to the taxicab that waited by the curve. As we drove away, I turned around and looked at my mother who stayed in front of the hotel, standing next to Carlota and waving goodbye. After I couldn't see her anymore, I looked down. Willy caressed my shoulder.

Sitting between his father and me, Phil kicked the back of the driver's seat and said he was hungry. Willy and I looked at each other, as we had already run out of food during the long trip.

About five minutes later, we arrived at the processing center, a one-story building that looked like a converted warehouse. When we entered, I was surprised to see the place packed with families waiting to leave. I later learned from the people sitting around us that they had come from different parts of the country.

As instructed, we sat down and waited for further instructions. Phil looked around with shyness and asked to go to the restroom. I was directed to one, and after we returned to our seats, he once again said he was hungry.

"There's nothing left," I said.

He looked down, as if he was about to cry.

"My love, if you love your daddy, you have to behave. Otherwise, they won't let us leave, and you know how much your dad needs this vacation," I told him.

He evaded my eyes and started to pull his fingers.

"Come on. Go to sleep," I said.

He shrugged and looked around the room.

About an hour later, an officer dressed in an olive-green uniform started to go around the room requesting passports and other documents issued by the Immigration Office. He collected them from everyone without any explanation.

After he went away, an elderly couple sitting near us complimented our son. Another woman who heard he was hungry whispered to him, "Don't worry. When you arrive in the United States, you will be able to eat a big meal." Phil looked at her with a tired look on his face. After a while, bored and hungry, he fell asleep in my arms.

Our flight wasn't scheduled to leave until the morning, so we had to sleep on the chairs. My arms became numb, but I didn't want to wake up my son who was sleeping peacefully. Watching him like that reminded me of the baby I'd lost. I didn't know if I would ever return to his gravesite, but I would always carry him in my heart.

As I waited, I thought about my parents and my sister. I had not left Cuba yet, and I already missed them.

"Are you okay?" Willy whispered, as if he had noticed my sad expression.

"I'm leaving all of my family behind," I said.

Chapter 29 – Saying Goodbye

He smiled and placed his hand on my shoulder. "You'll see them again soon," he said. "Besides, my family is your family."

Our conversation woke Phil who once again said he was hungry. He had not eaten anything since lunch, and when I said I had no food to give him, he began to cry.

A few minutes later, the elderly woman sitting next to me whispered a few words in her husband's ear. He nodded. She then reached into her bag and took out a can of condensed milk.

"For your child," she said, handing it to me.

"But...what about you and your husband?"

"We have another one. Don't worry."

I thanked her, and she gave me a can opener and verbal instructions on what to do. I was to get some water from the faucet and fill half of a cup, then pour some of the milk into it. This way the milk would last longer.

I left Phil with his father, asked one of the workers at the center for a cup, and went to the bathroom to get the water. Later, when I handed Phil a cup of milk, his eyes sparkled. After taking a sip, he said to his father and me, "Get some milk!"

It surprised me how much he cared for us at such a tender age. As hungry as we were, we decided to wait until our papers were cleared. I wasn't sure how many more hours we would spend at the processing center, or whether we would have to return home, so we stored the leftover milk to give to our son.

Each hour that followed felt like an eternity. I washed my face a couple of times and drank water from the faucet to numb the pain in my stomach. Willy, accustomed to being hungry while at the camp, didn't have as difficult a time as I did.

Sometime after ten, Phil fell asleep in my arms, and the morning found us like that, my arms numb from the lack of circulation, Phil surrendered to dreams without a care in the world.

In the early morning, two hours before our scheduled flight, an officer began to go around the room distributing passports.

"You and the boy can't leave on this flight," he said when it was our turn. "Only your husband can go."

Willy and I looked at each other. He knew what I was thinking and shook his head from side to side. He then directed his gaze back to the officer.

"Why?" Willy asked.

"Their names are not correct. When the first flight arrives in Miami, they will work with United States Immigration office to correct the spelling. If the names are corrected, you might be able to leave on the eleven o'clock flight, but there are no guarantees."

"Just go," I said. "If you don't leave, who knows what will happen to you. You're sick. Please go."

"No! I'm not going anywhere. I'll wait."

184

Chapter 29 – Saying Goodbye

After my insistence led nowhere, our wait resumed.

The first flight left after eight, taking most of the elderly and the families with children. We were the only family with a child who stayed behind. Phil became restless. He kept asking for his grandparents. When I said they were back home, he asked if he could play outside. To distract him, I gave him the leftover milk, and two hours later, he once again complained that he was hungry. This continued for a while.

When it was close to eleven, someone near us said cheerfully, "Look! Our airplane is landing!"

Willy squeezed my hand. I embraced my son with my free arm, closed my eyes, and prayed.

Moments later, an officer began to provide instructions to the people in the room. Two or three men from the Swiss Embassy returned passports to the travelers before allowing them to walk outside to the airfield. When they handed us ours, I held my breath.

"Come on. Keep moving!" Willy whispered when he noticed the confused look on my face. We began to walk, following other passengers outside. While we waited on the runway, Willy whispered in my ear, "You see? Everything is okay."

I didn't say anything, but I feared they would not let us leave.

Chapter 29 – Saying Goodbye

My legs trembled as we approached the metal stairs. I climbed first, followed by Willy, who now carried Phil in his arms.

Halfway up, I stopped for a moment to look at the door of the airplane. Almost there. I couldn't believe we were this close to freedom and convinced myself that something would occur to force us back down. I bowed my head and prayed.

"I'm hungry," my son said.

"You'll have to wait," Willy said.

When we were inside the airplane, I sat down by the window with my son on my lap and Willy by my side. The next few minutes lasted a lifetime.

I looked around at the other passengers and noticed their nervousness, from their empty gazes around the plane, to the way they avoided eye contact with the other passengers and the crew. Some had shadows beneath their eyes, but all appeared exhausted. Most of the people in this flight were adults, half of them in their fifties and sixties.

After everyone sat down, silence reigned. I could feel the blood rushing to my head and experienced shortness of breath. Willy noticed it and patted my shoulder a couple of times. When, at last, the airplane took off, a sense of relief overcame me. Then, the thoughts of those I'd left behind emerged.

"Goodbye, son," I said inside my head to the baby who would forever rest in Cuban soil.

I couldn't contain my emotions after that.

Chapter 29 – Saying Goodbye

My son glanced up at me and placed his tiny hand on my face.

"I'll be good, Mamá. Don't cry. I won't say I'm hungry anymore."

Chapter 30 - Free

Narrator: Madeline

The passengers cheered when the airplane's wheels touched down on the runway at the Miami Opa Locka Airport.

"Thank you, God! Free at last," yelled a teary-eyed middle-age woman, giving me chills.

Wide-eyed, we looked outside the windows while waiting to deboard, and once we did, smiling faces and tears poured onto the runway. After collecting our luggage, an airport officer separated Willy from my son and me and led him to a room for debriefing, while women and children were transported to a large old house, which may have been a hotel, judging by the number of rooms. The room assigned to us included two beds but no bathroom.

Since the moment we arrived, my son became restless, asking for his father, and marching around the room. I gathered a change of clothes for him and a fresh towel that had been left on the bed and looked for an employee who could help me find the nearest restroom.

A young woman led me to a large bathroom that included a tub. It was the first time Phil had seen one, and he examined it with distrust.

I placed him in it, turned on the shower, and let him play with the water, hoping it would help him relax. When he finished, I dressed him with a clean pair of slacks and a short-sleeve shirt that made him look like a little man, and we walked back to our room holding hands.

"Did you like the shower?" I asked.

"Yes," he said with a smile. For the rest of the afternoon, he played with imaginary trucks and asked me questions about his father.

Around six, Willy returned, tired from the long interview. Phil ran to him and hugged him.

"My dad is here!" he said, while his father patted him on the head.

Willy and I could not sit down to talk because moments later, through loudspeakers, we heard the announcement that everyone needed to report to the dining room.

We followed a group of men and women, many of whom I recognized from our airplane, to a large room furnished with a long table that accommodated over thirty people. When my son saw all the food that a server placed in front of him on a plate large enough for an adult—rice, black beans, salad, and the largest steak we had ever seen—he began to applaud and laugh. I cut his steak into tiny pieces and he devoured it. He then began to socialize with all the other families, asking them endless questions.

"What's your name? Where are you from? Do you have any kids?" This continued until his father signaled him to stop.

The next day, one of Willy's Miami relatives picked us up and took us to his home. In Miami, we immersed ourselves in the life of a cozy neighborhood near Calle Ocho ("Eighth Street"). I liked listening to people speaking in Spanish, gathering at the cafés to engage in conversations about Cuba, watching dozens of friends and neighbors coming to greet us, treating us as if they had known us all our lives.

Three days later, we flew to New York's John F. Kennedy International Airport.

It was October 23, 1969. The soft snow fell on the ground and on our bodies as we descended to the runway. It was cold but seeing snow for the first time invigorated me and somehow made me feel at home.

I grew with anticipation as we dashed towards the building. The moment the electric doors opened, my mouth opened wide as I heard the screams and laughter from the large group of family members and strangers that welcomed us with open arms. There were hugs, tears, kisses, and introductions. When I saw Willy's brothers and parents embrace him, I felt lonely and a little jealous.

I forced a smile, greeted everyone, and we talked for a while. The relatives soon began to argue with each other about who we would stay with. Everyone offered their homes. Cirilo, the one who had helped us get out of Cuba, won the argument.

The next day, Cirilo organized a big party at his apartment in Brooklyn with dozens of his friends. There was salsa music, dancing, lots of food, and even an opera singer. Little Phil ran around, danced, talked, and ate like he never had before.

Two weeks later, Enrique found us a second-floor apartment on Prospect Street in Port Chester, New York. For a few dollars, the previous tenant left us some of his furniture, and we began our life in this sleepy town near most of Willy's brothers and his parents. I couldn't believe that even the poorest people in this town lived better than those considered middle class where we grew up. People threw away so much usable stuff that it wasn't difficult to furnish an entire house with what others considered trash.

Happiness surrounded our family. It was a time when Beatles' music played on the radio, jobs abounded, and large family gatherings and church encompassed our life. Port Chester was a magical place: thirty minutes away from New York City, affordable, cozy, and close to Stew Leonard, our standard weekend-stop in Norwalk, Connecticut.

Phil loved to go through the grocery store in awe, asking for everything that caught his eye, from the giant apple pies to the apples, peaches, and pears arrayed in a festive display. Before we left, we always bought an ice cream cone for each one of us.

We ate so much in the months that followed our arrival to New York that after a while, I no longer looked like the girl Willy had met in Arroyo Blanco. I would stand in front of the mirror in disbelief of all my curves.

"I need to lose weight," I would tell my mother-in-law.

"*Mija*," she replied combining "my" and "daughter" in this endearing word. "That's the body grown men like. You look like a real woman, *hecha y derecha*."

Although I thought I lived in the best place on Earth, the news portrayed a different reality: protests throughout the country and a social transformation that threatened to bring the country towards the left.

Willy told me one night, "If those socialists understood, if they had lived for a day in my shoes, they would never protest against this great country."

"What makes this country great is the ability of everyone to speak their mind freely," I said.

He waved his hand in dismissal.

"I can't believe that you, of all people, would take their side."

"I don't, my love. You don't understand."

"*I* don't understand! No one understands what's happening more than I do. Don't think that because I didn't go to college, I don't see what's going on."

192

Chapter 30 - Free

It was no use arguing with Willy. His face would turn very red and his fists would close in frustration. The years we lived under a socialist system, and the time he spent at the forced-labor camp had scarred him more than I'd thought.

On November 15, 1969, after Willy returned from his job at Arnold Bakery, we ate dinner and sat on the sofa to watch the evening news on our black and white television. Parading through our screen, we saw half-a-million people who had gathered in Washington D.C. to protest the Vietnam War. Willy watched the report in silence. After a while, he took a deep breath, got up, and said, "Let's go to bed."

"Can I stay here watching the news, Dad?" our four-year-old asked.

"No, you go to bed too."

Phil crossed his arms and stomped his feet as we walked to his room.

A source of argument at our house, other than politics, was whether I should stay home and care for little Phil or work. Willy insisted that a man should provide for his family, while a woman should stay home raising her children. However, I wanted to work, like the other women in the family. I just didn't know who would care for my son.

One Saturday morning, when I shared my frustration with my mother-in-law Inés, she replied, "Find a job, sweetheart. Help your husband. Don't tell this to anyone, but Phil is my favorite grandson. He's an angel. I would love to care for him."

Chapter 30 - Free

It was settled. Inés began to care began to care for Phil, and I started to work for GAF Corporation sewing a variety of products made of felt. I was so happy to have a job. After a while, I worked very fast and became one of the fastest producers, which allowed me to make big bonuses.

I thought often of my sister and my parents in Cuba and made a promise not to rest until I saved enough money for us to be reunited.

Chapter 31 – Complications

Narrator: Madeline

On May 31, 1970, I cleaned the house like I did every Sunday. When I finished, I stood in front of Willy and sought his approval by turning my hands upward, as if asking "what do you think?" He hugged me and gave me a kiss on the cheek. "Spotless," he said.

He too did his part to help around the house, always fixing something. I was about to sit down on the sofa to take a break when the doorbell rang.

"Sit down," he said. "I'll get it."

Moments later, Willy swung the front door open and said, "What a surprise! What are you guys doing here this early? But please come in."

I smiled when I saw Willy hugging his brother Rolo and Rolo's wife, Maritza.

"Hola!" I said cheerfully, rose from the sofa, and walked towards them. "Please sit down. I'll bring you some coffee."

"No, don't bother. We just had coffee," said Willy's brother. "We won't be long, but I decided to come see you when I heard the news."

Chapter 31 – Complications

Willy, Rolo, and Maritza sat on the plastic-covered sofa and I on the chair across from them.

"What news?" I asked him.

He hesitated. "You haven't heard?" Rolo asked.

"No, what happened?"

"Well... Castro has decided to stop allowing people to leave Cuba."

"He what?" I asked. Abruptly, I stood up and brought my hands to my chest. "Rolo, don't play like this," I said.

"I'm serious."

My legs felt weak. At age twenty-nine, I was unprepared to lose my parents and my sister to the whims of a capricious dictator.

"Rolo please tell me that's not true," I said.

"I'm sorry, Madeline," Rolo said. "That son-of-a-bitch doesn't think it is enough to destroy the island. Now, he wants to separate families too."

I dropped back into the chair and wept for a long while. The brothers watched me in silence while Maritza came over and patted me on the back.

When I managed to contain my emotions, I went into the kitchen to make coffee for everyone. I had to do something. Maritza followed me into the kitchen and began to talk about her children, but my mind was elsewhere. As if noticing my disinterest, she excused herself and joined her husband in the living room.

Chapter 31 – Complications

Once she disappeared, I thought about my sister's most recent letter. I had read it several times but had not responded to it yet. It read:

Dear sister:

I hope you and the family are doing well. I try to imagine all the pretty things you tell me in your letters: the snow covering the town like a blanket, the pretty white houses with front porches and gardens full of flowers in the summer, and the stores with shelves full of food. It's like you are living in a fantasy world.

Life is very different here, and it's only getting worse. The government is practically forcing Alexis to join the military. He wants nothing to do with this government, and you can imagine how he's feeling. The other day, he began to shake uncontrollably. I didn't know what to do. I hugged him and kissed him until he stopped. The doctor told me he had a nervous breakdown. So many people here are losing their minds. A couple of people Alexis knows ended their lives.

What's happening to our country, my sister? How could things get this bad?

I hope you can get us out of here soon. I miss you so much. I can't wait until the day I can hug you again. I will send you pictures of your baby niece soon. She's growing up so much. Alexis thinks she looks like me.

Take care of my handsome nephew Phil and Willy, the best brother-in-law in the world. Give them a hug from me. Until we see each other again.

Your sister, Madi.

My sister didn't know I would have given all my possessions to be able to have her in my life again. Our reunification, now on hold for an indefinite period, changed everything.

***

As I began to accept the idea that years would pass before I could see my parents and my sister again, I went on about my days. What else could I do?

Life in the United States seemed to move faster than in Cuba. Willy and I both worked nights, a shift that came with a higher hourly rate. That meant we had to leave Phil with his grandparents. As protective as we were of our son, it wasn't easy for either one of us to leave him, but we had dreams and goals for our little family and hoped to take advantage of all the opportunities our new life afforded us. Willy now understood that if I worked, our lives would improve more rapidly.

One night, while I worked at GAF Corporation in Greenwich, Connecticut, and Willy at Arnold Bakery in the same town, we didn't suspect what was happening at the tiny house in Rye, New York, where Phil's grandparents lived.

Chapter 31 – Complications

After finishing at the bakery, Willy picked me up, and we arrived home after midnight. We had not yet showered when the telephone rang.

"Madam," the female voice said in Spanish. She then identified herself as a police officer. "Are you Madeline Montes?"

I held my breath and realized something was wrong. She told me she was calling from a hospital in Port Chester where my parents-in-law and Phil had been taken.

"Oh my God! Please tell me my son is okay!" I cried.

I kept repeating these words like a mad woman, sounding more and more like my mother. Willy rushed over to me and took the handset.

"Our son, Willy. It's our son!" I said interlacing my fingers over my head.

Willy listened to the woman as she explained the rest of the story. A homeless man who had fallen asleep on the porch somehow managed to set the house on fire while my family slept. Everyone was in stable condition. The boy had undergone treatment for smoke inhalation. The officer asked us to meet her at the hospital, as she needed to ask us some questions. Without getting a bite to eat, we rushed out of the house.

Willy drove our white Pontiac, while I shook like a scared bird. We made it to United Hospital on Boston Post Road in five minutes.

In the middle of the night, the tan-colored façade of the tallest building in the Village of Port Chester looked imposing, almost scary. After parking on the dark and deserted parking lot, we dashed toward the front entrance.

A policeman waited for us in the front lobby. He explained that the house had suffered substantial damage. My mother-in-law's foot endured a minor cut when the firefighters forced her and my father-in-law out of the house. After being taken out of the burning house, Inés kept screaming to the firefighters in Spanish that her grandson was still inside, but they could not understand her.

After various unsuccessful attempts of communicating with emergency workers, my boy's grandparents tried to run back in, only to be stopped by the police. A neighbor who heard Inés's screams translated her words to the firefighters. By then, the house was engulfed in flames. One of the emergency workers went in through a window. Moments later, he came back out with little Phil in his arms.

Phil was in and out of consciousness for a while, but after treatment, he began to improve. When we saw him, Willy and I embraced him and gave him dozens of kisses. He looked scared, with his face soiled from the ashes.

My son and my in-laws had been placed on emergency room beds several rooms away from each other. His grandparents didn't know my son's condition or speak enough English to ask about him, so they feared the worst.

"It's my fault," Inés kept repeating in tears when she saw me. "We lived in a cheap home. We should've lived in a better place. I'm

so sorry. If something happens to my grandson, I will end my life. You already lost a baby,
and I could not bear you losing another because of me. I'm so sorry."

She sobbed with the sadness of a mother
who had just lost her son. It broke my heart to
see her like that. I explained to her what the
police had told me, but it took a while for her
to calm down.

After leaving the hospital, my in-laws,
now homeless, moved in with me for a few
months. For several days, following his dis-
charge from the hospital, Phil kept coughing a
black soot until he began to improve.

The fire united ourH family, making us
realize the fleeting nature of happiness. In the
weekend gatherings that followed, we danced,
enjoyed family meals, and celebrated life.

Chapter 32 – The Return

Narrator: Madeline

In 1979, the Spanish-language television stations in Tampa, Florida announced the latest news in the evening broadcast. *Los Viajes de la Comunidad* had started. In order to bring needed funds into the island to improve a collapsing economy, Fidel Castro began to allow Cubans to return to visit their families.

"Oye, did you hear that? Is it true?" I asked Willy, and he nodded.

The emotions poured from my eyes, as if the passage of time had turned me, to some extent, into my mother. By now, the girl from Arroyo Blanco, or White Creek, like I used to call my town when I was learning English in Cuba, had disappeared. At age thirty-nine, the hours of hard work, the anguish of being far away from my parents, my sister, and the place I once called home, and the constant worrying about my boys erased that girl.

Phil had lost his boyish look and evolved into a level-headed fourteen-year-old. Our twin boys, born in 1976 at United Hospital in Port Chester, New York, had just turned three. All

Chapter 32 – The Return

of Willy's brothers had moved from New York to Florida. Some lived in Tampa and some in Orlando, but as their families grew, so did the distance between the brothers.

Willy knew I had no choice but to visit Cuba on my own as he needed to stay in Tampa with our children and traveling to the island was expensive. He feared for my safety since he didn't trust the Cuban government. As difficult as it had been to leave the island, we both knew that returning posed serious risks. What if they didn't let me leave?

During the days I prepared for my return, my husband kept repeating the same promise. If the government didn't allow me to leave Cuba, he would go there and kill as many communists as he could, even if he lost his life in the process. He reminded me of Phil when his father was away working in the fields. "You're not going to kill anyone," I said. "You have to be a father to these children. Stop it!"

He looked at me and crossed his arms. "You think I'm kidding?"

Every time I saw him that angry, I would bring him a plate of his favorite dessert. My mother-in-law always told me that food was the way into a man's heart, and that had proven to be true.

The massive number of people who flew back to Cuba to see their relatives caused my papers to be delayed. It took almost three months before everything was ready, including the re-entry documents.

Chapter 32 – The Return

We left the twins with one of Willy's brothers, and Phil, Willy, and I drove to Miami. From there, I was scheduled to take a direct flight to Camagüey. The government only allowed me to bring a limited number of pounds, so I wore several pairs of underwear, two blouses, and two pairs of pants. I carried the clothes and medicine I brought my family in a long, zippered cloth bag called a *gusano*.

When I said goodbye to my son and my husband at Miami International Airport and walked away towards the airplane, I felt as if I had left a part of my heart behind. I turned around and waved at them a few times, watching the two most important men in my life standing a couple of feet away from each other.

Phil and I were close, but Phil and his father didn't share the same interests. Willy worked at Tampa Shipyards, a difficult job that required him to spend hours repairing ships under extreme heat. That job toughened him, especially after he saw one of his coworkers die from a heart attack. The job paid well, and Willy did what he had to do to provide for his family.

Phil didn't care about physical activities. He preferred to spend hours reading, a reason why his classmates called him "the professor" at school. Willy wanted Phil to be more like him, but Phil had inherited the qualities I admired about my father.

Phil and Willy occupied my thoughts until I entered the airplane. Then I focused on my new reality and my anticipation grew. Soon, I would be home. My anxious eyes scanned the faces of the other passengers. I noticed they shared my nervousness. The male passenger next to me, as if realizing how on-edge I was, began to ask me questions about my family. He talked throughout most of the flight, making the journey more bearable. I could hear some of the conversations going on around me, the introductions, the questions, and the curiosity about the events that united us. "What year did you leave? Where are you from? How many pants are you wearing?" Most conversations revolved around the answers to those questions.

Minutes before we landed, the pilot made an announcement that sent chills through me: "Ladies and gentlemen, we know it's been years since you last saw your land. In a few minutes, if you look down, you will see the aqua-green waters of the coast, in the area of Santa Cruz del Sur. You're almost home. Welcome back."

All eyes inside the airplane, full of emotion, looked in the direction of the closest window. My seat offered a perfect view of the geography below, as the words of Christopher Columbus, the Italian explorer, echoed in my ears: "Cuba is the most beautiful land that human eyes have seen." In all its splendor rested the land I longed to see, the place that lived within me and ran through my veins. The man who sat next to me, as talkative as he had been until now, wiped a tear.

Chapter 32 – The Return

"We're home," I said, but he couldn't respond and looked away.

Later, as I was going through Customs, a government agent confiscated a cassette player I had brought my sister. This act made the memories return and reminded me of the reasons I left.

Once I cleared Customs, I began to walk towards the exit. My legs trembled when I thought about my encounter with my parents and sister, but the events around me distracted me from my thoughts as the group of passengers who accompanied me arrived at the waiting areas, and hugs, screams, and tears overwhelmed the airport. A teenage boy embraced his father; a grandmother kissed her daughter, a sister hugged a brother and yelled "my little brother. I missed you so much!"

"Madeline," a female voice shouted. I recognized it and looked up. In the distance, I saw her running in my direction, wearing a pair of white pants and white sandals, her long hair bounced as she ran. My sister. My little sister. I didn't want to drop my heavy luggage, afraid someone would take it, but I walked faster, with a smile drawn on my face and eyes shrouded in tears.

I couldn't help noticing how beautiful she was. She had colored her hair lighter and had left her teenage body behind.

"My sister," I yelled as she approached me. I placed down the heavy gusano and we hugged. I wished that moment would have lasted forever.

Chapter 32 – The Return

"I missed you, my little sister," I said.

"Me too!" she replied. "Every night, I prayed for this moment."

As she held me tight, I recalled the words she repeated as a child when I arrived home a few minutes late, and she feared my mother's retribution. "Defend yourself, Madeline. Defend yourself."

I knew she always had my back.

Looking thinner than I remembered, Alexis approached me with a shy smile, welcomed me, and gave me a warm embrace.

He then picked up my luggage and drove us to the house he had built for my sister. As I looked around me, from inside's Alexis's old red truck, sitting next to my sister and Alexis, I noticed that not much had changed. The forests and pastures still dressed in lush colors and the skies wore its bluest suit, but many towns had vanished after the American businesses left and people went to the city or abroad.

The conversation with my sister and Alexis distracted me for a while, but after the truck parked in front of Alexis's house, and I saw my parents walk out, my mother holding on to my father's arm with one hand and blocking the sun from her eyes with the other, I wondered how I would find the energy to run to them. I trembled with happiness.

"Papá!" I shouted when I managed to jump off the truck. It took longer than I wanted for the word Mamá to sprout out of my mouth, but when it did, tears rolled down my face, as I saw that both had aged beyond their years.

I ran to them and filled them with hugs and kisses long overdue. My father had a skeletal thinness that worried me, and he didn't act with the assertiveness of his younger years. As talkative as Mamá was before I left, she couldn't speak. She caressed my hair, looked at me with loving curiosity, and wept. They both had white hair and wrinkles around their eyes.

They didn't tell me how much they had missed me. Their expressions said it all. As they were asking me about my trip, from the corner of my eye, I saw a girl and a boy coming out of the house and approaching us shyly. They dressed in simple clothes, the girl with a sleeveless white dress, her black curls falling over her shoulders. The black-haired boy wore a white pair of shorts and a white undershirt. I recognized them from the pictures Nancy had sent me. The ten-year-old girl looked just like Nancy at that age, and the eight-year-old boy resembled his father.

"My beautiful niece and handsome nephew," I said with a wide smile and opened my arms to embrace them.

The smell of soil, the sight of the plantain trees near the house, and the sound of a rooster crowing reminded me of the home I once had. The notion that I would have to leave my family behind in only one week already felt unbearable.

Chapter 32 – The Return

After a while, dozens of family members and neighbors joined us and inundated me with questions. They didn't treat me the carefree way they did when I lived in Cuba. They didn't act like themselves around me, and looked at me with undeserved admiration, always anxious to please me in every way. I didn't want them to treat me that way and did everything possible to show them that even though I dressed in different clothes, I had not changed. Yet, no matter how hard I tried, that barrier, that perception that time had erased the old Madeline stood between my family and me like a painful reminder that nothing would ever be the same.

After dinner, when all the neighbors had left, I began to distribute the gifts I had brought my family. I gave my niece, Evelyn, several dresses. Her eyes shone with such happiness I wished I had been able to bring more. Moments later, she disappeared in the back of the house and came back with something wrapped in a piece of *cartucho* paper. She handed it to me and looked at me with excitement as I unwrapped it.

"A gift for me?" I asked.

She nodded.

When I saw a piece of used soap, I did everything I could to contain my tears.

"She kept a piece of the soap she used to bathe herself for you," her mother said. She wanted you to use the same soap.

I gave my niece a hug and thanked her for her thoughtful gift.

Chapter 32 – The Return

In front of me stood a child who had nothing, sometimes, not even soap, but felt inclined to share the little she had with me.

Chapter 33 – My Visit

The day after my arrival to my sister's house, I traveled with my her and her family to La Finca Estrella, the farm that housed my paternal grandfather's old home, and the place where I would be staying for the rest of my time in Cuba.

On the way, I noticed that if it weren't for the fewer people who lived around these parts, time had stood still, as if the video of Cuba's history had been placed on pause. The loud engine sound, coming in through the rolled-down windows, and the warm wind caressing my ears, made the conversation with Alexis difficult throughout the bumpy ride. Most of the way, we traveled on dirt roads lined with shrubbery or small country houses. I kept looking towards the back to make sure Nancy and her children were fine, as they had insisted on sitting on the floor of the truck's bed.

A relative had taken my parents to their home the previous night, so Mamá could prepare a big feast for the family. I begged her not to worry, but I knew her well. I gave her money so she could buy what she needed in the black market, as the food she could purchase with the ration card wasn't enough to feed her and Papá, never mind a large group of visitors.

As we entered the farm that my grandfather used to own, which the government nationalized in the 1960s, it seemed neglected and forgotten, so different from the vibrant and productive lands that were a source of pride for my grandparents.

Government workers had removed most of the *mamey*, mango, and avocado trees my grandfather's workers planted. They had hoped to cultivate the field with sugarcane, but due to mismanagement and lack of knowledge, that never happened, so weeds took over the empty, unattended land, while two tractors parked on the edge of the field rotted.

As the truck drove through the dirt road, it lifted dust up in the air. Mamá must have seen the truck through her window because by the time we parked in front of the house, she and my father stood on the porch waving at us and smiling. It was still early, and the morning sun illuminated the small parcel of dew-moistened vegetables that surrounded the house. My parents had taken advantage of the land the government allowed them to keep, and their garden looked lush and healthy, in contrast with the poor conditions that reigned over the rest of the farm.

Chapter 33 – My Visit

In two more hours, my grandparents' house would be full of family like it was when they lived there. We would eat fresh chicken with rice, beans, and potatoes, while their spirits accompanied us. Mamá thought that although they had died, they never left the farm. She thought they watched over their family, the few who lived in Arroyo Blanco and in the southern portion of Camagüey. She thought that as long as one of their children and grandchildren lived, they would watch over them.

Mamá outdid herself with her cooking. Sitting around the large dining room table or anywhere they could find a place to sit, relatives talked and laughed after lunch. I liked to see the house so full and vibrant.

Even Tía Rosita came to visit. Her hair had turned grey, but she seemed as energetic as when she used to play with Sultán on my grandparents' porch.

Everyone engaged in conversation, except for my father. He sat in a corner of the dining room and didn't talk much. After a while, he glanced at me, rose from his chair, and walked towards the back of the house. I excused myself and followed him into the bedroom he shared with Mamá. He sat on a chair and me at the edge of the bed across from him.

He lifted his head, and his eyes, hidden behind thick lenses, met mine. "We haven't had a chance to talk," he said. "I'm glad you came. I just needed a couple of minutes alone with you. I hope that's okay."

Chapter 33 – My Visit

"Of course, it is, *mi viejito*. I missed you so much." I paused for a moment, doing everything possible to hold back the tears. "Why don't you let me claim you and Mamá again? You look so unhappy here."

"I can't leave your sister and her children here. You know that. She needs me more than you, especially now that she has two kids. I would never ask you to claim everyone. It's too expensive." He paused for a moment, looked down, and then focused his eyes on me once again. "I won't lie to you... Living in this place is killing me. You know how hard I worked, how hard my parents worked to leave their family the fruits of their labor. To see how all that hard work became meaningless in an instant was something I wasn't ready to face. When this government decided to take our land to do with it as it wished, it was as if they had erased your grandparents and me. They made all our sacrifices meaningless."

His head turned in the direction of the bedroom's door. I concluded he wanted to ensure no one was listening.

"You have not been erased Papá. No one can ever do that. Look at the big family you and Mamá created. Doesn't that count for something?"

"*Mija*, you don't understand. A man can't live without freedom."

He remained quiet again.

"You know? The funny thing is that this move of allowing people to visit their families after so many years will have consequences

214

they haven't anticipated. They made a big mistake."

"What do you mean?"

"Look at how you're being treated!" he whispered. "Your visit is opening many eyes that until now had been closed. When a blind man hasn't seen the light, he doesn't miss it because darkness is all he knows. But if you give him a glimpse of it, he can no longer live without it. The government took everything away from you when you left. Now, you're coming back, telling us about the amazing life you live. It has nothing to do with material things, although, of course, that helps, but you have the freedom to travel practically anywhere in the world. You can buy a house if you want to. Private property is respected in the United States. You can say anything you want about the government and nothing will happen to you. Your visit is showing people that while this government has destroyed our old Cuba, those who were lucky to leave prospered in a capitalist country. You are proof that communism doesn't work. It's against the very fiber of human beings.'"

I had listened attentively to my father, nodding throughout his monologue, realizing how much he needed to say what he was feeling. Then I took a deep breath. I too feared that someone could be listening, so I decided to change the topic.

"So, tell me, Papá, have you visited Arroyo Blanco recently? I miss my old town."

"The last time I did, it was unrecognizable. Nothing is what was, so I stopped going there. Our town has been erased."

Hearing his words saddened me, but I didn't want to show him that. "Come on, *mi viejo*. No more talking about this government. I'm here with you now, and that's what counts. I want you to be happy. Life is too short."

He smiled and nodded. Our conversation then shifted to my children, the family I left behind, and the plans I had for the future. I could see his eyes glistening when I told him about the house that Willy and I had purchased for the twins and Phil. I showed him recent pictures of them, and he asked if he could keep them.

"Of course, Papá," I said. "Anything you want."

Chapter 34 – A New Reality

Narrator: Madeline

My sister and Alexis only knew about life in the United States through my letters, but Castro's propaganda had clouded their understanding. Castro's government controlled everything: the media, the means of production, and everyone's lives. I too knew little about the new Cuba that throughout the years had grown closer to the Soviet Union.

Nancy's children sang Russian songs and the communist anthem *The Internationale*. Their teachers told them that those who had left Cuba betrayed the motherland. Nancy called these tactics brainwashing, and as much as she tried to counter what her children learned at school, she felt she was losing the battle. Her children showed me what would have happened to my son if I had stayed. Like them, he would've lived in darkness, disconnected from the rest of the world.

During my short stay in Cuba, despite the constant traffic of relatives coming in and out of the house and endless conversations that took the form of questioning sessions, I managed to observe the interaction between

Nancy and Alexis. They were perfect for each other. He held her hand when they walked outside and looked at her with such tenderness that I felt a sense of relief. I knew he would never allow anyone to harm her. She responded to his love with shy and playful looks and little pushes when he glanced at her for too long.

Before my trip, Alexis and Nancy already wanted to leave Cuba, and my conversations with them about life in the United States only reaffirmed their desire. Unfortunately, the rules would have required them to travel to Spain first, a complicating factor given their young children and my aging parents. Also, Alexis's parents had no plans to leave. When Alexis's mother learned about her son's desires, to my surprise, she told him: "If you leave me to go to Spain, I hope your plane disappears at sea. It will be less painful to know you're dead."

After considering all the facts, Alexis decided it would not be a good idea to leave, which condemned my parents to staying in Cuba.

During the time I spent in Camagüey, it never occurred to me to visit my son's grave. I told myself I didn't have enough time, when my desire not to relieve the past dictated my actions.

I didn't see my old friend Mirta during my trip. I heard she had moved away. Many of the people I remembered from my childhood, like Migdalia, the woman who delivered babies in

Arroyo Blanco, had vanished from these parts never to be heard of again.

On the day of my departure, everyone who knew my parents, or who'd learned from others about my visit, came to say goodbye. I never expected to see what I witnessed that day. People lined up in a long row along the dirt path that my cab took after leaving my parents' house. Men, women, and children, communists and those who opposed the government, all waved goodbye and smiled. Judging by the number of people, it appeared as if the entire town and those from surrounding areas had joined the crowd. I saw in their expressions a longing for a different life, an admiration for me I didn't deserve.

Inside the taxi, Alexis and Nancy, who shared the back seat with me, voiced their surprise as they saw government sympathizers treating me like a foreign dignitary.

"For the first time in years, the town is united. You did this, Madeline," Alexis said.

I didn't agree with him. I was the spectacle of the moment. After my departure, I knew everything would return to the old way.

During the trip to the airport, Nancy held my hand and glanced at me as if she didn't want me to leave.

"Don't forget to write and give my nephew a hug for me," she said. "Tell him I love him. Kiss the twins for me."

I nodded. She then caressed my hair and looked at my outfit.

Chapter 34 – A New Reality

"You didn't have to wear my old dress, you know?" she said.

Alexis glanced at my clothes for a moment. I had left the ones I brought and my shoes behind and wore one of my sister's outfits that had seen better days.

"Are you kidding, Nancy? Why not? Now she looks like one of us."

"What's wrong with that?" I asked.

"Come on Madeline. Look at us. We look like zombies. There are two types of Cubans, those who have lost their minds and those who have turned into zombies."

The driver, a friend of Alexis, shook his head. Alexis said a couple of more jokes about life in Cuba, but I noticed he was more careful, as if he were afraid the driver would report him. As we approached the sign "*te quiere y abraza* Camagüey," located outside the airport, a simple phrase that welcomed visitors, Alexis stopped talking.

Afraid the driver would tell the wrong person about Alexis's comments, I insisted in paying him in dollars, a more valuable currency than the peso that would go farther in the black market. The driver's eyes lit up, and he assured me that he would always be at my service if I decided to return.

Later, when I hugged Alexis and my sister goodbye, Nancy shed a tear.

"I'll be back, my little sister. We'll see each other again soon."

She nodded and her eyes focused on the airport's polished floors. Not knowing when I would be able to return to Cuba, I gave them a final embrace.

Later, as I walked away, I thought about the past few days. Although Cuba had remained stuck in time while the world kept moving forward, the fiber of its people had changed. People's fears had made them accepting of their new reality.

I discovered that I no longer belonged in Cuba. Those who stayed behind now considered me an outsider and referred to the place where I lived as "your country." However, I felt like an outsider in the United States, in part because I had traveled there as an adult and didn't master the language. If I didn't belong in Cuba or in the United States, where then?

I learned that when I traveled abroad, I stopped belonging to one place or another and became a citizen of my memories.

Chapter 35 - Graduation

Narrator: Madeline

Since our arrival in the United States, we had experienced three different administrations: Nixon, Ford, and Carter, the first two Republican and the last Democrat. Each had its own focus and perspective about the economy and social welfare and its own set of challenges. Yet no matter who was in power, the country marched forward. Cuba, on the other hand, remained in the past, with its crumbling buildings and a stumbling economy.

Castro kept promising better times, but as the years passed and promises remained unfulfilled, people's patience began to evaporate. The opening of Cuba to those who had abandoned it years before lifted the veil off the eyes of those who stayed behind, which led to the inevitable events that followed.

In 1980, the Washington Post published an article describing how a group of Cubans "rammed their way to embassy grounds in a stolen bus." They asked the Peruvian Embassy in Havana for political asylum. When embassy officials refused to turn in the offenders, Castro retired his guards from the entrance, which resulted in thousands of Cubans flooding its grounds. The events that ensued led to one of the largest exoduses in Cuban history: the Mariel boatlift.

That year, President Jimmy Carter allowed over 120,000 Cubans to come to our shores. Some people in the United States were not happy about this move, while others welcomed the refugees with open arms. My son Phil, who turned fifteen when the exodus started, joined the people who gathered at the McFarlane Park in Tampa to support the refugees, not knowing that the girl who would one day become his wife was one of the refugees. It didn't take long for the massive number of immigrants to overwhelm the immigration authorities, which ultimately led to the end of the exodus in October of the same year.

Three months later, in 1981, President Reagan came to power. He became a popular president and one of my husband's favorites, given his foreign-policy goal of rolling back world-wide communism. A year later, Phil met Tania, a Cuban refugee, through a blind date. Knowing Tania changed my son. He seemed more interested in learning about Cuba and talked about her often. She attended Jefferson High School and he Tampa Bay Tech, but their paths had crossed when one of Phil's friends began to date Tania's younger sister. Phil fell in love with Tania the moment he saw her. The blond Havana girl who had come from Cuba in 1980 also captured my love and sympathy, but

Chapter 35 - Graduation

I feared my mother's reaction, as Tania's family was just starting out in America, while we had achieved more financial stability.

Tania's parents had been kept apart by the Cuban government for almost twelve years, her father in the United States and her mother, along with their three children, in Cuba. The reintegration of the family had faced various challenges. The father turned into an alcoholic during the years the family remained apart, and the girl's grandmother faced depression after she had to leave her husband and sisters in Cuba.

Despite all the obstacles, Tania was a good student, and Phil began to focus more on his grades as they competed with one another about which one would graduate with a better grade-point average. In the end, they both did well.

I never graduated from high school, so when Phil announced, in 1983, he had met all the requirements to graduate from Tampa Bay Tech, I could not be happier. His graduation also coincided with my parents' long-anticipated visit to Tampa.

In April, less than two months before his graduation, Phil turned eighteen. A model son—thoughtful, caring, and loving—Phil had made motherhood a joyful experience, but I felt that his time to leave home was near.

My parents arrived from Cuba a couple of days before Phil's graduation, an emotional reunion that allowed them to see Phil after so many years and Phil's twin brothers for the first time.

The visits to the grocery stores, so full of everything my parents could ever want to eat and the ability to speak without fear impacted my father on a deep emotional level. Sometimes, he couldn't contain his tears in front of me.

"What's wrong, Dad?" I would ask him.

"If your sister could only be here. This is the most amazing country in the world."

On graduation day, Willy drove my parents, the twins, and me to the USF Sun Dome, the place that would house the event, while Phil went to pick up his girlfriend and her family.

On the way to graduation, as my parents sat in the back seat of the car, Dad looked at the city going by while I glanced at him through the rearview mirror. He wore a long-sleeve shirt, the same type he wore when I was growing up. His hairline had receded since the last time I saw him, but he still enjoyed a full head of white hair.

"Are you happy, Dad?" I asked, turning my head in his direction.

He nodded.

"If only your sister and her family could be here," he said.

"Happiness is seldom complete, Dad."

"It's good to feel free at last," he said. "But you know what's interesting? After living under Castro's Cuba for twenty-four years, I'm still afraid to say how I feel. I'm afraid that no matter where I go, someone will always be watching."

His words made my blood boil.

"You should stay here, Dad," I said as we headed north on Interstate 275.

"We can't," my mother replied, shaking her head. "You know how I feel about your sister. She's my pride and joy and needs us. I can't leave her and my grandkids. I would rather die."

Although I recognized the truth in her words, I felt a little jealous about her preference for Nancy.

"Parents are always more protective of the child who needs them most, Madeline," my father said, as if he had interpreted my silence. "When I was raising you, I never expected you to turn into one of the strongest women I know. I'm proud of you, my daughter, and what you have done with your life. I'm sorry you've had to work as hard as you have."

Afraid Willy would find offense in my father's words, I realized I needed to act.

"Dad, my husband has been a great provider. He risks his life every day to feed and clothe his family. I'm lucky to have him."

"You misunderstood, *mija*," he replied. "As parents, we always want our children to have a comfortable life. I didn't raise you to clean floors and bathrooms at a school, like you're doing, but I understand that times have changed. Women now have to leave their children in daycares to help their husbands."

"We're also immigrants, Dad, and don't speak English well. Our sacrifices were never meant to benefit us but our children. Today, my dream is coming true. My son is the first person in our family to graduate from high school, but this is only the beginning. He speaks English well and is bright. I hope he goes on to college and has a great life."

Later, as we sat on the bleachers waiting for Phil to walk across the stage to receive his diploma, my father reached for my hand and held it tight. Like with every graduation, the energy and emotions of the day, the ending of a chapter and start of the next, united a massive room of strangers. People from multiple backgrounds, each representing a dot in the great collection that constitutes humanity, converged on this special occasion to celebrate a new beginning.

After the numerous caps and gowns emptied the main stage, the relatives followed the graduates outside the Sun Dome. There, under a bright summer sun, the congratulations and hugs began.

We kept looking around, trying to find Phil and his girlfriend Tania. At last, I saw his glasses and thin mustache, complemented with a smile that brightened the afternoon. I alerted Willy and my parents, and we rushed towards him. He looked so happy next to Tania and her family.

Tania had just graduated from high school herself and had registered to start the university in the fall. Her smile concealed her history and far-from-perfect life, but that didn't matter, only the way that Phil and Tania looked at each other did. I saw in her that same girl from Arroyo Blanco that Willy fell in love with many years before.

My mother seemed to like Tania as much as she liked Willy when she first met him. I didn't see it at the Sun Dome but later, when we joined Tania and her family at her house for a celebration. As little as they had, they bought my son a cake and sodas. I could tell by the way my mother stared at Tania that she felt Tania wasn't good enough. The girl wore donated clothes that didn't fit properly and appeared malnourished, but she worked hard to gain my mother's sympathy. She hugged her and kissed her, like she would her own grandmother. Yet, judging by my mother's serious expression, nothing Tania could do would persuade Mamá to change her mind.

On the day my parents were scheduled to return to Cuba, we received a call from Tania.

"What's wrong, sweetheart?" I asked when I picked up the handset.

At first, Tania could not get a word out.

"It's my grandmother," she said at last. "She's dead. She shot herself."

Tania's grandmother had left her husband in Cuba, not Tania's grandfather, but the man she married several years after she lost her first husband. The reunification with her son in the United States, after the Cuban government kept the family apart for twelve years, resulted in the sudden separation from her husband and sisters. She was not even able to say goodbye to him, as he was at work when the authorities came to pick her up.

I asked Phil to go to Tania's house. She needed him more than I did. Meanwhile, Willy, the twins, and I accompanied my parents to Miami.

During our trip, I kept hoping my parents would change their minds and stay. I needed them more than they thought, but it wasn't meant to be. In the end, their desire to protect my sister won.

Chapter 36 - Reunion

Narrator: Madeline

My father used to tell me that sometimes God compensates us for the things he takes away. My first gift came to me one night, after I received a frantic call from Tania, "My Dad just found out I was pregnant and threatened to kill Phil! Please tell him to come get me. I ran away."

"Tania, calm down, sweetheart. He must be bluffing," I said.

"He had a gun in his hand!" she replied. "I got scared and left."

Her words left me speechless. Phil, who stood only a few feet away from me, as he was helping me clear the table, must have read my expression. He walked towards me and took the handset away.

"Tania, what's going on?" he asked. After he spoke to her, he ran out of the house like a madman.

Chapter 36 - Reunion

That same night, Tania arrived at my house with only the housedress she was wearing. When she walked into our living room, she looked frightened. I hugged her, and she wept in my arms. We sat together and spoke for a long time.

She spoke for a long time. She had suffered more than I had imagined. Her mother attempted suicide when Tania was six. Tania came into her mother's room just in time to stop her, but the experience had scarred her for life. She told me about the twelve years her parents had been apart because the Cuban government didn't allow her mother, Tania's siblings, and Tania to leave Cuba. Tania's eyes showed such sadness I felt compelled to help her.

"Don't worry, sweetie. Everything will be okay," I said.

Tania and my son held hands and exchanged glances. I saw in them the angst I had when my parents took me away from Willy. I sensed then that God had sent me a gift by bringing Tania into our lives, but I didn't know how precious it would be.

Two days later, Phil and Tania went to the justice of the peace to get married. The judge and his secretary served as witnesses. No one in her family attended the ceremony, and both Willy and I had to work.

Tania, the 98-pound girl, would not be able to see her father or her siblings again for several months, not until my grandson was born.

After Tania left her house, her father had told her siblings, "Your sister has died today. Her name will not be mentioned in this house again."

He didn't anticipate that the birth of his first grandson, seven months later, would make him change his mind. He didn't understand he had no control over whom Tania loved, the same way my parents couldn't control how I felt about Willy.

A few months later, Phil's son, Phil Jr., would once again bring the family together. He was my second gift.

***

After the birth of my first grandson, the passage of time brought me many joys and sometimes tears.

Seven years passed since my parents' visit to Tampa, and the economy in Cuba continued to deteriorate. Desperate to take my parents out of the island, I never thought I would have to pay such a heavy price for our eventual reunification.

On December 15, 1990, I called my sister to check on my parents. She said Dad had been very sick but was feeling better.

"When are you coming back to Cuba?" she asked.

Chapter 36 - Reunion

"I don't know, Nancy. There's a lot going on in the world. I should probably wait a little longer. Why?"

"It's just that... I've been having some bad dreams lately. I'm afraid we will never see each other again."

"How can you say that? One should never say such things. Of course, we will. You need to have faith."

"I stopped having faith a long time ago," she said. "Just know that whatever happens, I'll always watch over you, you hear?"

"Stop talking like that!"

"Don't mind me, sister. You know what they say about the people who stayed in this God-forsaken island: whoever isn't crazy is getting there."

"Nancy, please take care of yourself and the rest of family. Give everyone a hug, okay?"

"I will."

"We'll talk again in the New Year, you hear me?"

"Okay, Madeline. Kiss everyone on my behalf."

After the call ended, I shared our conversation with Willy, but he said I shouldn't worry.

"People in Cuba need to get closer to God," he added.

However, I just couldn't stop thinking about her words.

On December 31st, my Tampa family and I welcomed the New Year at my son's new

house in Carrollwood. By then, he and his wife had purchased a four-bedroom, two-bathroom home. For years, they worked full time and attended college in the evening, which led them to graduate with their bachelor's degrees.
Now, they were working on their master's degrees at the University of South Florida.

On the evening of January 1st, 1991, Tania's parents joined us at our house for dinner. Rio, Tania's father, who by this time had lost all his hair, made us laugh like I had not laughed in years when he put on a man's wig and spoke to us in silly voices. He played Monopoly with Phil Jr. and made Pepito jokes. Pepito was the personification of the Cuban tragedy, a fictional, misbehaved child who asked difficult questions of his teachers without the filters of adulthood. Pepito became the therapy of the Cuban people, who took refuge in comedy to escape reality.

"Let me tell you another," Rio said. "Listen, listen... Pepito is in class, and the teacher asks all the kids: 'Can you share any personal news with the other students?' Pepito raises his hand and says: 'Yes, professor. My dog had three puppies, and they are all revolutionaries.' The professor is glowing with happiness. Two weeks later, some high-ranking officials come to visit, and the teacher asks the same question. This time, Pepito raises his hand again and says enthusiastically: 'Yes, professor. My dog had three puppies, and they all want to go to the United States.' Outraged, the teacher asks: 'But two weeks ago, you told me they were revolutionaries.' Pepito replies: 'Yes, professor, but they opened their eyes.'"

I had never laughed as hard as I did that night, but the occasional recollection of my sisters' words kept me on edge.

We welcomed the New Year with twelve grapes, wine, and music. I thought about calling Cuba but decided to wait until the morning. When I did, no one answered. I tried again the next day. No answer.

On January 3rd, when I finished ironing the twins' school shirts, the telephone rang. Willy answered and moments later, he handed me the handset. "It's your mother," he said.

I squinted at him and placed the handset against my ear.

"Mamá? Is everything okay?"

The words I heard shook me to the core.

"Oh Madeline...! I've lost her!"

As I heard her sobbing, I tried to process what she meant.

"Mamá, please explain what happened! Who are talking about?"

"She didn't suffer," Mamá said. "She died instantly."

"Who died, Mamá?"

I imagined, judging by her reaction, that it had to be one of my older aunts. However, when she finally answered my question, my world stopped. I couldn't breathe. Everything started to spin around me, and I let out a scream. Willy rushed to me. He pulled a chair and asked me to sit down.

"What happened, Madeline?"

I couldn't answer him at first. When he saw me bring my hands to my chest, he rushed to the refrigerator and brought me a glass of water.

"Drink," he said. "And please let me what's going on!"

"It's my little sister, Willy!" I said, dropping my head on my lap. Willy embraced me and kissed my head.

"Oh my God!" he said.

"She was only trying to help," I explained. "But then a drunk driver came and took them both."

Willy tried to take the handset, but my mother was still explaining what happened. The night had fallen, and Nancy, Alexis, and two policemen searched with flashlights for an object that one of the policemen had lost in the grass. The details were sketchy, confusing. All four of them were standing by the side of a deserted country road. They saw the lights of the approaching vehicle but continued to search. Within minutes, the driver shattered their lives after losing control of his Jeep. Drunk, he had fallen asleep at the wheel.

By the time Nancy was taken to the hospital, she was already dead. Her husband had survived the accident, but when he woke up and saw her bloody and lifeless body next to him, he suffered a heart attack.

Chapter 36 - Reunion

As my mother spoke, I recalled Nancy's dream. Nancy died the way she had lived, helping others. A Castro policeman would be the last person she helped.

***

I returned to Cuba one last time. By then, whatever had been left of the girl from Arroyo Blanco was dead and buried with my little sister.

Unlike my first trip, this time I visited my son's resting place, but it wasn't until I stood in front of my sister's gravesite that I lost my composure and questioned God for taking her so soon. She didn't deserve to die, nor did Alexis.

If a heaven did exist, I hoped Nancy and Alexis had gone there. The lives they'd lived made them deserve heaven. In their deaths, I hoped my baby son had gained a mother and a father.

With my sister's departure, my parents lost what tied them Cuba. I felt guilty, as if my wishes had led to this. I would have given all I had to save my sister, even my life. I also felt guilty that in my desire to take my parents out of Cuba, I would cause Nancy's children to lose their grandparents. I consoled myself with idea that they were now adults and had their paternal grandparents in their lives, while Dad kept getting more frail by the day. I needed to get him out before it was too late. I wanted him to die as a free man.

Chapter 36 - Reunion

Life in Cuba worsened following the dissolution of the Soviet Union on December 26, 1991. The Special Period (or *Periodo Especial*), a deepened economic crisis, followed, after Cuba lost approximately 80% of its imports. Power outages, long waits at bus stops, hunger, and malnutrition became an everyday reality.

Life in the United States was also changing. In 1993, President Bill Clinton won the presidency. My husband wasn't happy, as he equaled democrats with socialists. No one could make him understand that the two weren't equivalent.

Once Clinton took office, it seemed as if all Willy could talk about was the mistake that the American people had made by voting him into office, but I had no patience for politics. Every time he started an emphatic monologue about the new administration, I would go into the kitchen.

Sometime after Clinton's inauguration, we received a call from Cuba. My parents had received the approval to leave the island. As much as I had anticipated this day, the thought of my dead sister clouded my happiness.

On the day of my parents' expected arrival, Phil rented a Dodge minivan and took his wife, his nine-year-old son, Willy, and me to Miami International Airport. During the five-hour trip, I felt anxious, not knowing if my father could survive the emotions of the trip.

Phil Jr. made the time go by fast by singing the "Ghost Busters" and "Love Shack" songs and making jokes.

I never imagined that I would love my first grandson as much I loved Phil, Jr., or that Tania would become the daughter I didn't have. They helped me through my long grieving process: Phil Jr., by grabbing my face every time he saw me sad and forcing me to smile, and Tania, by listening to my stories about my sister. Tania loved to write, but back then, I didn't realize it would be Tania who would one day write my story. Through the pages of that book, my sister would live again.

We arrived at Miami International Airport before noon and waited. Phil Jr. began to tell me a story about one of his teachers when a woman who sat next to me began to scream.

"My sister! Oh, dear God, thank you for bringing you after all these years."

The woman ran to her sister and embraced her. As they did, I looked down. Moments later, I felt a tap on my shoulder.

"Mamá," Phil said. "Grandma and Grandpa are here."

I looked up in the distance and saw their confused faces. Mamá carried most of the luggage. After all these years, she still cared for my father, but the man I knew would never have allowed her to carry all that weight.

"Papá!" I yelled. "Mamá!"

We all rushed towards them. I first embraced my father, then my mother. Meanwhile,

Phil took her bags and Willy grabbed my father's. A few seconds later, my mother let go of my embrace.

"Oh my God!" she said. "Is this my great-grandson? I can't believe how much he's grown."

With tears in their eyes, she and my father embraced the boy and kissed his cheeks.

"He looks just like your son at that age," Papá said.

As he extracted a handkerchief from his pocket and wiped a tear, I noticed the additional wrinkles on my parents' faces.

"It's over, Papá," I said, placing my arm around him. "Your nightmare is over. You're finally free!"

"Thank you, Madeline for allowing me to live in a free country before it's too late."

"Come on, mi viejo," I said. "I'll take good care of you, and you'll live for many more years."

We walked outside together, me holding the hand of my eighty-seven-year-old father, my eighty-one-year-old mother holding on to his arm.

After that day, we stayed busy every weekend showing my father what it was like to live in America. We took them to the movies, to grocery stores, and to our neighbors' houses. We also drove them to Orlando to visit Willy's brothers. Willy's family welcomed them with a big meal and treated them like their own parents. During the celebration, my father kept looking at me without saying a word. I knew what he was thinking.

One Saturday afternoon, we drove to Clearwater Beach to watch the sunset. Dad looked enthralled by his surroundings. After the sun disappeared on the horizon, he took a deep breath and squeezed my hand.

"Thank you," he said.

Every night, when we returned home from work, he would thank Willy and me for allowing him to experience freedom after so many years without it. Then one sunny afternoon, after he finished reading the newspaper on the porch, he came inside the house and sat next to Willy. My husband was watching Sábado Gigante, one of his favorite television shows.

"I never told you this," my father said. "Do you remember that I didn't want you to marry Madeline?"

Willy lowered the volume, turned to my father, and nodded.

"She was a girl, and I was too stubborn to listen to her," my father added. "However, now that at the end of my life, it's important not to leave any words unsaid. Willy... thank you. Thank you for making my daughter so happy all these years. Thank you for being true to your word and caring for her. I can die in peace knowing she has you by her side."

His voice cracked as he said this. Lately, he had become more emotional than usual when recounting the past.

"No reason to thank me, sir. It's been an amazing journey."

My father pressed his lips together, patted Willy on the hand, and nodded.

That evening, my father hugged each member of his family goodnight and told us how much he loved us.

"Thank you for letting me experience life in a free country," he said, as he had said so many times after his arrival.

Mamá accompanied him to his bedroom, took out his clean pajamas from a drawer, and helped him get ready for bed. After watching a television program, the two of them fell asleep in each other's arms.

My father never woke up. God took him into his arms that night. The next morning, while we waited for the ambulance, Mamá cried inconsolably, but she wasn't ready to join him yet. Stubborn as always, she had to wait for the twins to become men, for one of them to give her two great-grandchildren. She needed time to love them and to see them grow up.

Mamá was the most caring of great-grandmothers, always sharing what she had with her great-grandchildren and loving them until her heart had no more love to give.

She held on to life with the fierceness of a lioness. When her body could no longer sustain her, and her legs collapsed under the weight of the years, she asked her mother to take her home.

Chapter 36 - Reunion

Tania, the girl she didn't love at first but who became a granddaughter to her and a daughter to me, helped me care for Mamá during her final moments of life. It was Tania who closed her eyes. Mamá had just turned 101 years old, the end of a life well-lived.

One day, Tania, by documenting our story, would give eternal life to a girl who once lived in Arroyo Blanco.

And now, as Willy and I enjoy our last years of life together, I know that wherever my parents are, Papá is still holding Mamá's hand. I know that the two of them, Alexis, and my sister are caring for my baby son. They left me to start a new happy life in heaven and will wait until the girl from Arroyo Blanco joins them again.

Pictures

Nancy and her husband

Sign outside the airport on my first visit to Cuba

Credits and Acknowledgements

I would like to thank all the following people for their incredible help in assembling the information that would form the basis of this novel, or for reading and telling others about my books:

My mother, Milagros, for dedicating her life to her family, advocating for/ education, and showing me the importance of giving back to the community.

Maria Fernandez, for always being a mother to my siblings and me and all her support.

My husband and friend, Ivan, for his patience and support throughout the writing of this book and his invaluable suggestions regarding key sections of the manuscript. Thank you for writing the paragraphs in the back cover.

To my son Ivan and his wife Gloria for all their support.

Kayrene Smither, a reader and friend who offered to read my draft and always has excellent recommendations. I am so grateful for her friendship and feedback.

Shelly Corzo Shaffer for being one of my beta readers and offering her suggestions.

My loyal friends and readers, too numerous to mention, for sharing my posts, reading my books, and telling others about them.

Credits and Acknowledgements

My mentor, Professor John Fleming (University of South Florida Creative Writing program) to whom I am indebted for his teachings and support.

Madeline Viamontes and her husband Guillermo for trusting me to document their story, for being like parents over 35 years, for answering questions about life in Cuba prior to and after Castro's revolution, and for cooking lunch every weekend during the final months of the writing of this book. Thank you, Madeline, for helping me with the translation into Spanish.

My sister, Lissette, and my brother, René, (and their children) for their encouragement and for telling people about my books. Also, to Jeff, my sister's husband, for all his support.

All my extended family, too numerous to mention, and to people who, although not blood relatives, have become family. Tracey O'Neil, my other sister, thank you!

My growing number of readers around the world, and to the book clubs that have selected my books. Thank you for supporting independent authors.

Kimberly Ruiz, author of the wonderful children's book *The Magic Glove* and her husband Rico Ruiz, for their suggestions on the cover.

The wonderful Facebook group Women Reading Great Books for helping me decide whether to include titles for each chapter.

MigrationPolicy.org for an insightful article.

Credits and Acknowledgements

https://www.migrationpolicy.org/article/cu-ban-migration-postrevolution-exodus-ebbs-and-flows

PBS.org for this helpful article.
https://www.pbs.org/wgbh/americanexperi-ence/features/post-revolution-cuba/

The History Channel, for the videos and footage about Cuba.

About the Author

Betty Viamontes was born in Havana, Cuba. When she was fifteen years old, she and her family boarded a shrimp boat off the coast of Havana during what became known as the Mariel boat lift. Over two hundred refugees accompanied her that stormy night when many people perished on similar overloaded boats. Since the family arrived in Key West in 1980, Betty's mother told everyone: "One day, my daughter will write our story." Betty's parents have passed away, but in 2015, Betty fulfilled a promise she made to her mother by publishing the novel *Waiting on Zapote Street,* based on the story of her family. Her novel was selected by the Gulf Coast Chapter of a United Nations book club for its February 2016 reading and has been presented at a local university due to its historical relevance. One of its chapters appeared in the 2016 USF literary journal *The Mailer Review.* Her short stories and poems have been published in literary magazines, anthologies, and newspapers. She is a speaker and holds graduate degrees in business administration and accounting from the University of South Florida, from where she also received a Graduate Certificate in

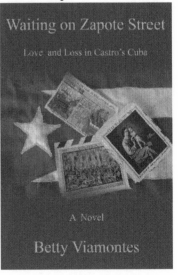

Creative Writing. She published the anthology *Candela's Secrets and Other Havana Stories*, the novel *The Dance of the Rose*, a sequel to *Waiting on Zapote Street*, and the novel *Havana: A Son's Journey Home.*

In 2018, *Waiting on Zapote Street* was a winner at the Latino Books Into Movies Award, Drama TV Series category, an award chaired by the talented actor Edward James Olmos.

Betty is working with three other authors (Susana Jimenez Mueller, Jean Morciglio, and Anna Brubaker) on *Like Finding Water in the Desert*, an anthology that hopes to inspire other women around the world.